WeightWatchers®

$1

Winner's Circle

145+ FAVORITE RECIPES
FROM MEMBERS, LEADERS,
AND HOME COOKS

A WORD ABOUT WEIGHT WATCHERS

Since 1963, Weight Watchers has grown from a handful of people to millions of enrollments annually. Today, Weight Watchers is recognized as the leading name in safe and sensible weight control. Weight Watchers members form diverse groups, from youths to senior citizens, attending meetings virtually around the globe. Weight-loss and weight-management results vary by individual, but we recommend that you attend Weight Watchers meetings, follow the Weight Watchers food plan, and participate in regular physical activity. For the Weight Watchers meeting nearest you, call 800-651-6000. Also, visit us at our Web site: **weightwatchers.com.**

ICON KEY

HOT/SPICY

NO COOK

ONE POT

20 MINUTES OR LESS

VEGETARIAN

WEIGHT WATCHERS
PUBLISHING GROUP

Creative and Editorial Director
Nancy Gagliardi

Art Director
Ed Melnitsky

Production Manager
Alan Biederman

Office Manager and
Publishing Assistant
Jenny Laboy-Brace

Food Editor
Eileen Runyan, M.S.

Recipe Consultant
Maureen Luchejko

Photographer
Dasha Wright

Food Styling
Michael Pederson

Prop Styling
Cathy Cook

Designer / Illustrator
Julia Michry

Designer / Production
Lynda D'Amico

On the Cover: Southwestern Layered Salad, page 80 (with a **POINTS**® value of only 3)

Contents

Introduction

When I first started working on books for Weight Watchers, one of the first in-the-works projects I inherited was a cookbook compiled from a recipe contest we publicized in *Weight Watchers* Magazine. The concept: Send us a favorite recipe that you created to help you lose weight. I remember when the responses started pouring in—our offices were filled with boxes and boxes of submissions, and someone was hired for a year to specifically work on that project. I came in at the fun part of the job—when the winners had to be chosen (read: I got to taste a lot of the recipes!). From there we designed, photographed and produced the book. *Weight Watchers Simply the Best* became one of our best-selling cookbooks and, in fact, still is.

I remember spending that year reading quite a few of the entry forms filled with notes that people submitted with their recipes. Some of the criteria for the recipes were that they had to be delicious enough to serve to family, friends, and company (no "diet food" allowed); and they had to be relatively easy. The ingredients were quite sophisticated. Also, the one thing I read over and over from the entrants' forms was that no matter how simple the recipe, if it didn't taste great, what was the point of making it?

Those entries helped me create a foundation for the countless cookbooks I would go on to produce for Weight Watchers. They helped me understand what was truly important to those who were struggling with losing weight while trying to cook for themselves and their families.

Seven years later we decided to revisit the concept—we think with resounding success. Thus, *Weight Watchers Winner's Circle* comes to you, as did its predecessor, from a contest we ran in *Weight Watchers* Magazine—the September 2002 issue in this case. In came the entries, and we hired someone to work on the project (note: she didn't get the whole year because we wanted to get the book to you ASAP!). And, again, I got to taste and taste and taste and read and re-read. My thoughts on how America cooks, circa 2003? The recipes range from elegant to homey; they are even speedier than before, and the ingredients are even more sophisticated. The one thing that remains unchanged: They all taste great!

Enjoy,
Nancy Gagliardi
Creative and Editorial Director

CHAPTER 1

Appetizers

HOT AND COLD GREAT BEGINNINGS

Cabbage-Wrapped Shrimp with Wasabi Cream

Susanne Santos, Napa, CA

These sushi-like rolls are bursting with delicious flavor. "My husband is a meat-and-potato guy. He doesn't like sushi, which I love," says Weight Watchers member, Susanne. "But he does like this dish, so it makes us both happy."

¼ cup fat-free sour cream

2 tablespoons light mayonnaise

1 teaspoon wasabi paste

⅛ + ¼ teaspoon salt

1½ cups water

⅔ cup jasmine rice

1 (8-ounce) package frozen cooked salad shrimp, thawed and coarsely chopped

1 medium seedless cucumber, peeled and diced

½ ripe avocado, peeled, pitted, and diced

¼ cup chopped fresh cilantro

2 scallions, finely chopped

1 tablespoon fresh lime juice

8 large leaves savoy cabbage, Swiss chard, or Chinese cabbage, tough ribs removed

6 tablespoons reduced-sodium soy sauce

MAKES 8 SERVINGS

1. To make the wasabi cream, combine the sour cream, mayonnaise, wasabi paste, and ⅛ teaspoon of the salt in a small bowl. Cover and refrigerate at least 30 minutes or until ready to serve, up to 2 days.

2. Meanwhile, bring the water to a boil in a medium saucepan; add the rice and remaining ¼ teaspoon salt. Reduce heat and simmer, covered, until liquid is absorbed and rice is tender, about 15 minutes. Remove from heat and let stand 5 minutes. Fluff the rice with a fork then transfer to a large bowl to cool. Stir in shrimp, cucumber, avocado, cilantro, scallions, and lime juice; set aside.

3. Cook the cabbage leaves in boiling water until wilted, about 2 minutes. Drain and set aside to cool. Cut each cabbage leaf lengthwise in half. Working 1 leaf half at a time, place a scant ¼ cup rice mixture in the center of the bottom third of the leaf half. Fold over the sides then roll up from the bottom of the leaf to form a package. Repeat with the remaining leaves and rice mixture to make a total of 16 rolls. Serve with the wasabi cream and soy sauce.

PER SERVING (2 rolls with 1 teaspoon wasabi cream and scant tablespoon soy sauce): 138 Cal, 3 g Fat, 1 g Sat Fat, 0 g Trans Fat, 58 mg Chol, 689 mg Sod, 18 g Carb, 2 g Fib, 9 g Prot, 39 mg Calc. *POINTS* value: 3.

CABBAGE-WRAPPED SHRIMP
WITH WASABI CREAM

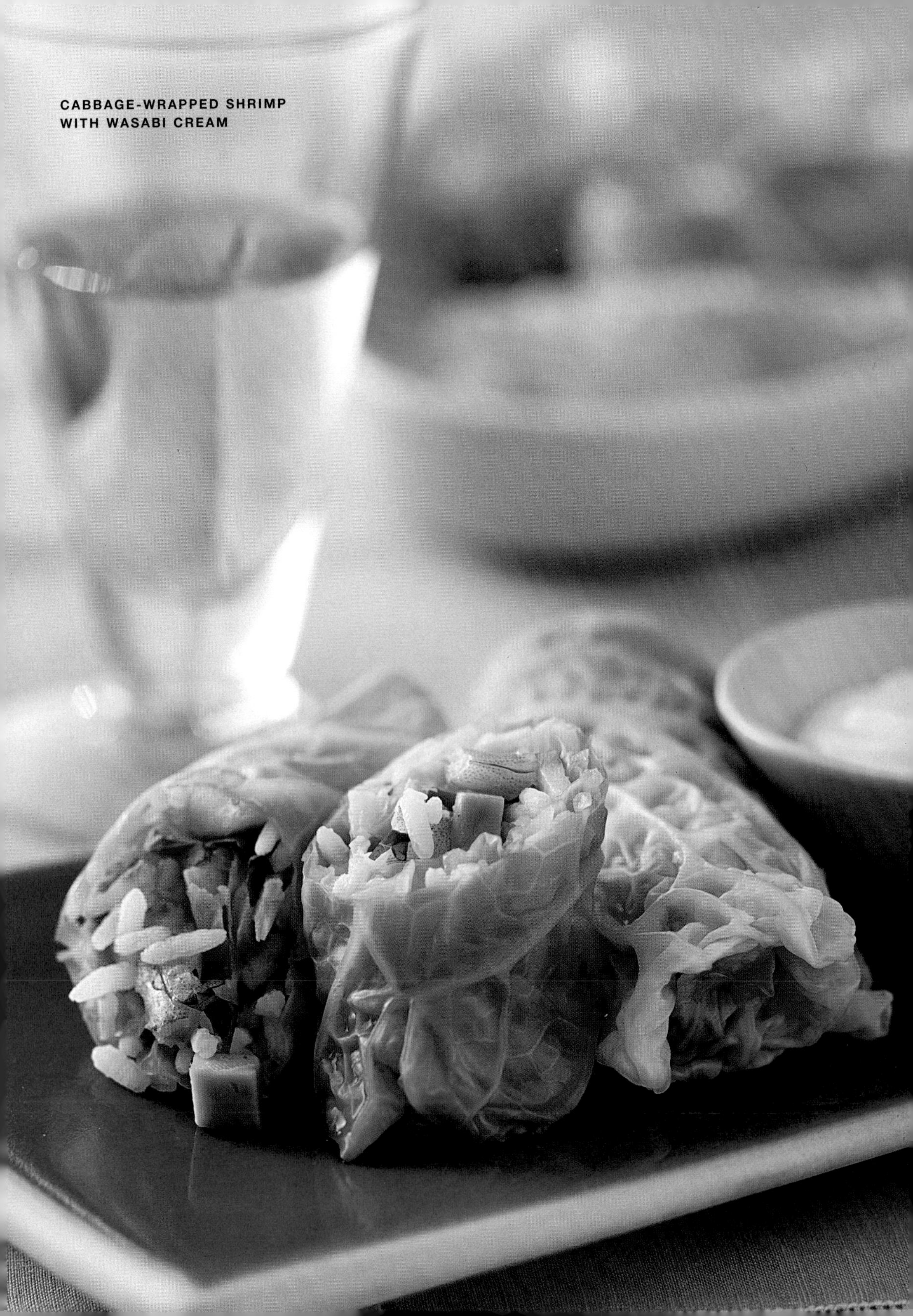

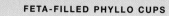

FETA-FILLED PHYLLO CUPS

Feta-Filled Phyllo Cups

Debbie Vanni, Libertyville, IL

Debbie typically serves these light and flaky tartlets at parties or large family gatherings. "People are always asking me for the recipe," she proudly proclaims. "I have fun with it—sometimes I change the kind of olives and herbs I use." The filling can be made a day ahead and kept, covered, in the refrigerator.

2 (2.1-ounce, 15-shell) packages frozen, fully baked mini phyllo dough shells

1 (4-ounce) package reduced-fat feta cheese crumbles

3 ounces fat-free cream cheese, at room temperature

¼ cup fat-free egg substitute

15 kalamata olives, pitted and chopped

2 teaspoons fresh lemon juice

1 garlic clove, minced

1 teaspoon all-purpose flour

⅛ teaspoon ground cumin

3 tablespoons chopped pimientos, drained

Parsley leaves, for garnish

MAKES 15 SERVINGS

1. Preheat the oven to 350°F. Arrange the phyllo shells in one layer on a 10 x 15-inch jelly-roll pan; set aside.

2. With an electric mixer at medium speed, beat the feta cheese, cream cheese, egg substitute, olives, lemon juice, garlic, flour, and cumin in a large bowl until smooth. Spoon about 2 teaspoons of the cheese mixture into each shell.

3. Bake until the filling is set and the tops are golden, about 15 minutes.

4. Top each tartlet with a few chopped pimientos and a parsley leaf. Serve at once while still hot.

PER SERVING (2 pieces): 78 Cal, 4 g Fat, 1 g Sat Fat, 0 g Trans Fat, 3 mg Chol, 220 mg Sod, 6 g Carb, 0 g Fib, 4 g Prot, 28 mg Calc. *POINTS* value: *2.*

APPETIZERS

Salmon Mousse

Linda Tilley, Manteca, CA

Linda, a Weight Watchers Lifetime member, says "Meetings motivate me to stay on target." Slimmed-down classics such as this, which she first made for her daughter's christening celebration, also help. Not only is it delicious and easy, it can be made up to two days ahead. If you like, serve with cocktail (party-style) rye bread (2 slices will increase your *POINTS* value by 1).

1 (6-ounce) can salmon, drained

⅓ cup fat-free mayonnaise

⅓ cup plain fat-free yogurt

½ small onion, grated (about 2 tablespoons)

1 medium dill pickle, chopped (about 2 tablespoons)

1 tablespoon chopped fresh dill

1 tablespoon fresh lemon juice

¼ teaspoon salt

¼ teaspoon freshly ground pepper

1 envelope unflavored gelatin

¼ cup cold water

1 bunch watercress, tough stems removed

1 small cucumber, thinly sliced

MAKES 8 SERVINGS

1. Pulse the salmon, mayonnaise, yogurt, onion, pickle, dill, lemon juice, salt, and pepper in a food processor until smooth.

2. Sprinkle the gelatin over the cold water in a small microwavable bowl and let stand until softened, about 5 minutes. Microwave the mixture on High until the gelatin completely dissolves, 30–40 seconds.

3. Add the dissolved gelatin to the salmon mixture and pulse until blended. Spoon the mixture into a 2½-cup ring mold. Cover and refrigerate until set, about 3 hours or overnight.

4. To serve, unmold the mousse onto a large platter. Surround with the watercress and cucumber slices.

PER SERVING (¼ cup mousse): 49 Cal, 2 g Fat, 0 g Sat Fat, 0 g Trans Fat, 13 mg Chol, 349 mg Sod, 4 g Carb, 1 g Fib, 5 g Prot, 74 mg Calc. *POINTS* value: **1**.

tip If you don't have a ring mold, spoon the mousse into a small bowl (2½ to 3 cup capacity) lined with plastic wrap. After unmolding the mousse, remove the plastic wrap.

Shrimply Delicious Deviled Eggs

Kris McAllister, Seminole, FL

"I am very proud of my success. This year I will be 50 and fit!" writes Kris, who has just reached her goal weight, having lost 28 pounds. She guarantees that if you serve these at your next party, "everyone will ask for the recipe!" You can find cooked salad shrimp in the freezer section of your supermarket. The recipe can easily be doubled for larger crowds.

6 hard-cooked eggs, shelled

6 ounces frozen cooked salad shrimp, thawed and finely chopped

3 tablespoons light mayonnaise

1 tablespoon Dijon mustard

¼ teaspoons seafood seasoning

1 tablespoon chopped fresh parsley

MAKES 6 SERVINGS

1. Halve the eggs lengthwise. Remove the yolks and save for another use. Set the egg whites aside.

2. Combine the shrimp, mayonnaise, mustard, and seasoning in a medium bowl. Spoon the shrimp mixture into the egg white halves. Sprinkle with the parsley. Place the eggs on a plate and serve at once. Or cover with plastic wrap and refrigerate until ready to serve, up to 2 hours.

PER SERVING (2 halves): 73 Cal, 3 g Fat, 1 g Sat Fat, 0 g Trans Fat, 58 mg Chol, 414 mg Sod, 1 g Carb, 0 g Fib, 10 g Prot, 18 mg Calc. *POINTS* value: *2*.

tip To make this deliciously different appetizer partially ahead, make the filling early in the day and store, covered in the refrigerator. Refrigerate the cooked egg whites in one layer in zip-close plastic bags. Assemble the eggs just before you're ready to serve them.

APPETIZERS

Avocado and Cream Cheese Tortilla Rounds

Ann Lovelace, Conroe, TX

"When I worked at our local high school, I was always asked to bring these pinwheels," remembers Ann fondly. We can see why—the filling is well flavored with avocado adding a rich creaminess as well as a lovely light green hue.

1 ripe avocado, peeled, pitted, and chopped

1 (8-ounce) package fat-free cream cheese, at room temperature

¼ cup canned sliced water chestnuts, drained and coarsely chopped

3 tablespoons fat-free Ranch dressing

3 tablespoons fat-free sour cream

2 scallions, thinly sliced

2 tablespoons sliced ripe olives, coarsely chopped

8 (6-inch) fat-free flour tortillas

1 cup prepared picante sauce or salsa

MAKES 16 SERVINGS

1. Pulse the avocado, cream cheese, water chestnuts, dressing, sour cream, scallions, and olives in a food processor until smooth.

2. Warm the tortillas according to package directions. Spread ¼ cup of the avocado mixture onto each tortilla. Roll up then cut each tortilla crosswise into fourths, making a total of 32 pieces. To serve, arrange the pieces cut-side up on a plate. Serve with the picante sauce.

PER SERVING (2 pieces and 1 tablespoon sauce): 77 Cal, 2 g Fat, 1 g Sat Fat, 0 g Trans Fat, 1 mg Chol, 335 mg Sod, 11 g Carb, 2 g Fib, 3 g Prot, 34 mg Calc. POINTS value: *1.*

tip Choose Haas avocados for an extra-creamy taste. You can identify them by their dark, rough-textured skin. To ripen hard avocados, place them in a fruit bowl on a counter or in a paper bag for two to three days.

Cheesy Bean Tortilla Rolls

Susan McElrath, Powder Springs, GA

The filling for this tasty little appetizer can be made a day ahead and the tortillas can be filled and rolled early on the day you plan to serve them. Simply cover the rolls with a damp paper towel then with plastic wrap and keep refrigerated. Slice them just before serving. For added flavor, use sun-dried tomato tortillas.

¾ cup canned black beans, rinsed and drained

½ cup shredded reduced-fat cheddar cheese

3 ounces light cream cheese (Neufchâtel), at room temperature

4 scallions, thinly sliced

½ red bell pepper, seeded and diced

1 jalapeño pepper, seeded and minced (wear gloves to prevent irritation)

6 (6-inch) fat-free flour tortillas

MAKES 12 SERVINGS

1. Mash the beans with a fork in a medium bowl. Stir in the cheddar cheese, cream cheese, scallions, bell pepper, and jalapeño pepper until blended.

2. Warm the tortillas according to package directions. Spread ¼ cup of the bean mixture onto each tortilla. Roll up then cut each tortilla crosswise into fourths, making a total of 24 pieces. To serve, arrange the pieces cut-side up on a plate.

PER SERVING (2 pieces): 120 Cal, 4 g Fat, 3 g Sat Fat, 0 g Trans Fat, 13 mg Chol, 272 mg Sod, 15 g Carb, 3 g Fib, 6 g Prot, 71 mg Calc. *POINTS* value: **2**.

FROM TOP LEFT, GINI'S PINWHEELS, AVOCADO AND CREAM CHEESE TORTILLA ROUNDS, CHEESY BEAN TORTILLA ROLLS, AND SALSA PINWHEELS

Gini's Pinwheels

Virginia C. West, Miami, FL

"I've been taking my pinwheels to get-togethers for years and have tried to change to something else, but my friends always insist I bring Gini's Pinwheels," writes Virginia, a Lifetime member who lost 34 pounds on the Weight Watchers program. When she can, she prepares these spirals ahead of time, arranges them on the baking sheet (without baking them), then bakes them at the site of the party so they are fresh when she serves them.

3 ounces fat-free cream cheese, at room temperature

4 slices bacon, cooked and crumbled

1 small onion, minced

1 (8-ounce) tube refrigerated, reduced-fat crescent dinner roll dough

MAKES 12 SERVINGS

1. Preheat the oven to 375°F. Spray a nonstick baking sheet with nonstick spray.

2. Combine the cream cheese, bacon, and onion in a small bowl until well blended.

3. Separate the dough to make 4 rectangles and arrange them on a work surface. Press the perforations together with your fingers to make 1 (8 x 13-inch) rectangle. Spread the cheese mixture onto the dough. Starting with the long side, roll up, jelly-roll style. Cut the roll, crosswise, into 24 ($\frac{1}{2}$-inch) slices. Using a small spatula, transfer the slices, cut-side up, about $\frac{1}{2}$ inch apart, onto the baking sheet.

4. Bake until puffed and golden, 10–12 minutes. Serve hot.

PER SERVING (2 pieces): 88 Cal, 4 g Fat, 1 g Sat Fat, 0 g Trans Fat, 2 mg Chol, 228 mg Sod, 9 g Carb, 0 g Fib, 3 g Prot, 14 mg Calc. *POINTS* value: *2.*

APPETIZERS

Salsa Pinwheels

Jane L. Josephs, San Diego, CA

Jane has lost over 31 pounds so far and credits the program and her "wonderfully supportive leader" for giving her the confidence to stay with "a sound and sensible eating plan." You can use any combination of veggies you like here—diced cucumber, chopped tomato, and chopped fresh spinach are all healthy choices.

½ cup fat-free cream cheese, at room temperature

¼ cup prepared salsa

½ green bell pepper, seeded and diced

½ red bell pepper, seeded and diced

½ red onion, diced

¼ cup chopped fresh cilantro

1 tablespoon fresh lime juice

4 (6-inch) whole-wheat tortillas

4 green leaf lettuce leaves

MAKES 12 SERVINGS

1. Combine the cream cheese and salsa in a small bowl until smooth; set aside.

2. Combine the green and red bell peppers, onion, cilantro, and lime juice in a medium bowl.

3. Warm the tortillas according to package directions. Spread one-fourth of the cream cheese mixture onto each tortilla. Top each with a lettuce leaf then evenly spoon on the bell pepper mixture. Roll up then cut each tortilla diagonally into sixths, making a total of 24 pieces.

PER SERVING (2 pieces): 60 Cal, 2 g Fat, 0 g Sat Fat, 0 g Trans Fat, 1 mg Chol, 167 mg Sod, 11 g Carb, 1 g Fib, 4 g Prot, 43 mg Calc. *POINTS* value: *1.*

Easy Curry Spread

Pamela Reed, Fremont, CA

Serve this deliciously different spread with vegetable crudités, toasted pita wedges, or your favorite fat-free crackers. To save time, you can substitute an equal amount of fat-free cream cheese for the yogurt cheese.

¾ cup yogurt cheese*
2 scallions, finely chopped
1 teaspoon curry powder
¼ cup mango chutney

MAKES 8 SERVINGS

Combine the yogurt cheese, scallions, and curry powder in a small bowl; spread the chutney evenly over the top. Refrigerate, covered, until the flavors are blended, at least 30 minutes or up to overnight.

PER SERVING (2 tablespoons): 34 Cal, 0 g Fat, 0 g Sat Fat, 0 g Trans Fat, 1 mg Chol, 28 mg Sod, 7 g Carb, 0 g Fib, 2 g Prot, 62 mg Calc. **POINTS** value: **1**.

tip To prepare yogurt cheese, spoon 1½ cups plain fat-free yogurt into a coffee filter or a cheesecloth-lined strainer; place it over a bowl. Refrigerate, covered, at least 5 hours or overnight. Discard the liquid in the bowl. Makes about ¾ cup yogurt cheese.

Tuna and White Bean Dip

Elisa Stasi, Pittsburgh, PA

Lifetime member Elisa likes to serve this protein-rich spread on slices of zucchini
or celery sticks. It's also good with warmed pita bread or sesame breadsticks.

1 (15½-ounce) can white
   beans, rinsed and drained

1 (6-ounce) can solid white
   tuna in spring water, drained

3 tablespoons chopped
   fresh basil

1 tablespoon fresh lemon juice

1 tablespoon extra-virgin
   olive oil

1 teaspoon capers, drained

1 garlic clove, chopped

¼ teaspoon salt

¼ teaspoon freshly
   ground pepper

MAKES 8 SERVINGS

Process the beans, tuna, basil, lemon juice, oil,
capers, garlic, salt, and pepper in a food processor
until smooth. Transfer the mixture to a serving
bowl and serve at once. Or refrigerate, covered,
until ready to serve, up to 1 day.

PER SERVING (¼ cup): 62 Cal, 2 g Fat, 0 g Sat Fat,
0 g Trans Fat, 7 mg Chol, 166 mg Sod, 6 g Carb,
2 g Fib, 6 g Prot, 23 mg Calc. *POINTS* value: *1*.

Spicy Curry Dip

Cathy Saynuk, Baltimore, MD

Toasting the curry powder releases the fragrance and flavor of this pungent spice and adds a significantly different taste to the dip. Cathy likes serving this with strips of bell peppers, cucumbers, celery, carrots, and scallions.

½ cup fat-free mayonnaise

½ cup reduced-fat sour cream

2 tablespoons minced onion

1 tablespoon ketchup

1 teaspoon Worcestershire sauce

1 garlic clove, minced

4 drops hot pepper sauce

1 tablespoon curry powder

MAKES 10 SERVINGS

1. Combine the mayonnaise, sour cream, onion, ketchup, Worcestershire sauce, garlic, and hot pepper sauce in a small bowl.

2. Toast the curry powder in a small dry skillet over low heat, stirring constantly, until fragrant, 1–2 minutes. Stir the curry powder into the mayonnaise mixture. Refrigerate, covered, until the flavors are blended, at least 30 minutes or up to overnight.

PER SERVING (2 tablespoons): 57 Cal, 4 g Fat, 1 g Sat Fat, 0 g Trans Fat, 5 mg Chol, 131 mg Sod, 4 g Carb, 0 g Fib, 1 g Prot, 23 mg Calc. *POINTS* value: *1.*

Roasted Chili Salsa

Gina F. Rodreguez, Santa Maria, CA

"If you like, add chunks of ripe avocado to this yummy salsa, just don't forget to up the *POINTS* value!" writes Gina. One avocado is worth 8 *POINTS* value, giving this appetizer a *POINTS* value of almost 1.

3 medium tomatoes, cut into fourths

5 medium tomatillos, cut in half (discard papery husks and rinse tomatillos before halving)

1 large onion, cut into 1-inch-thick wedges

3 garlic cloves, chopped

½ cup chopped fresh cilantro

1 or 2 small dried red hot chile peppers (such as chiles de arbol or Thai chiles), seeded (wear gloves to prevent irritation)

1 tablespoon cider vinegar

¼ teaspoon salt

MAKES 12 SERVINGS

1. Preheat the oven to 450°F. Spray a large nonstick baking pan with nonstick spray.

2. Combine the tomatoes, tomatillos, and onion in a large bowl; lightly spray with olive-oil nonstick spray. Spread the vegetables in the baking pan. Roast, stirring occasionally, until the vegetables are tender and lightly browned, about 45 minutes. Remove the pan from the oven and let the vegetables cool to room temperature, about 20 minutes.

3. Transfer the vegetables, in batches, to a food processor. Add the garlic, cilantro, chile pepper, vinegar, and salt; pulse until smooth. Transfer to a serving bowl and refrigerate, covered, until ready to serve, at least 30 minutes or up to 3 days.

PER SERVING (¼ cup): 16 Cal, 0 g Fat, 0 g Sat Fat, 0 g Trans Fat, 0 mg Chol, 149 mg Sod, 4 g Carb, 1 g Fib, 1 g Prot, 6 mg Calc. *POINTS* value: **0.**

tip To seed dried chile peppers, simply pull off their stems and shake out the seeds. Find dried hot chiles in the ethnic section of your supermarket. They'll last up to one year in an airtight container in a cool, dry place.

Baked Sauerkraut Balls

Jane McCormick, North Canton, OH

Jane makes these ahead of time and freezes them in zip-close plastic freezer bags. As she needs them for holidays (they are a family favorite on New Year's Eve) or other gatherings, she simply transfers them to a saucepan and simmers them, covered, until they are completely heated through.

1 teaspoon canola oil

1 pound sweet Italian turkey sausage, casings removed, sausage crumbled

1 (14.4-ounce) can sauerkraut, rinsed, drained, and finely chopped

1 (8-ounce) package fat-free cream cheese, at room temperature

½ cup plain dry bread crumbs

MAKES 15 SERVINGS

1. Heat the oil in a large nonstick skillet over medium-high heat. Add the sausage and cook, breaking it up with a wooden spoon until browned, about 10 minutes. Remove from the heat. Stir in the sauerkraut and cream cheese until blended. Transfer the mixture to a large bowl. Cover and refrigerate until chilled, about 45 minutes.

2. Preheat the oven to 350°F. Spray a nonstick 10 x 15-inch jelly-roll pan with nonstick spray.

3. With wet hands, shape the sausage-sauerkraut mixture into 30 (1¼-inch) balls. Place the bread crumbs on wax paper. Roll the balls in the crumbs to coat evenly. Place in a single layer without touching each other on the jelly-roll pan. Spray lightly with nonstick spray. Bake until browned, 25–30 minutes. Serve at once.

PER SERVING (2 sauerkraut balls): 73 Cal, 2 g Fat, 1 g Sat Fat, 0 g Trans Fat, 19 mg Chol, 394 mg Sod, 5 g Carb, 1 g Fib, 8 g Prot, 44 mg Calc. **POINTS** value: 1.

tip To reheat in the microwave, simply transfer half a batch of the frozen meatballs to a microwavable dish and microwave on High until heated through, stirring once, about 6 minutes.

SPICY PARTY MEATBALLS
WITH MANGO-YOGURT SAUCE

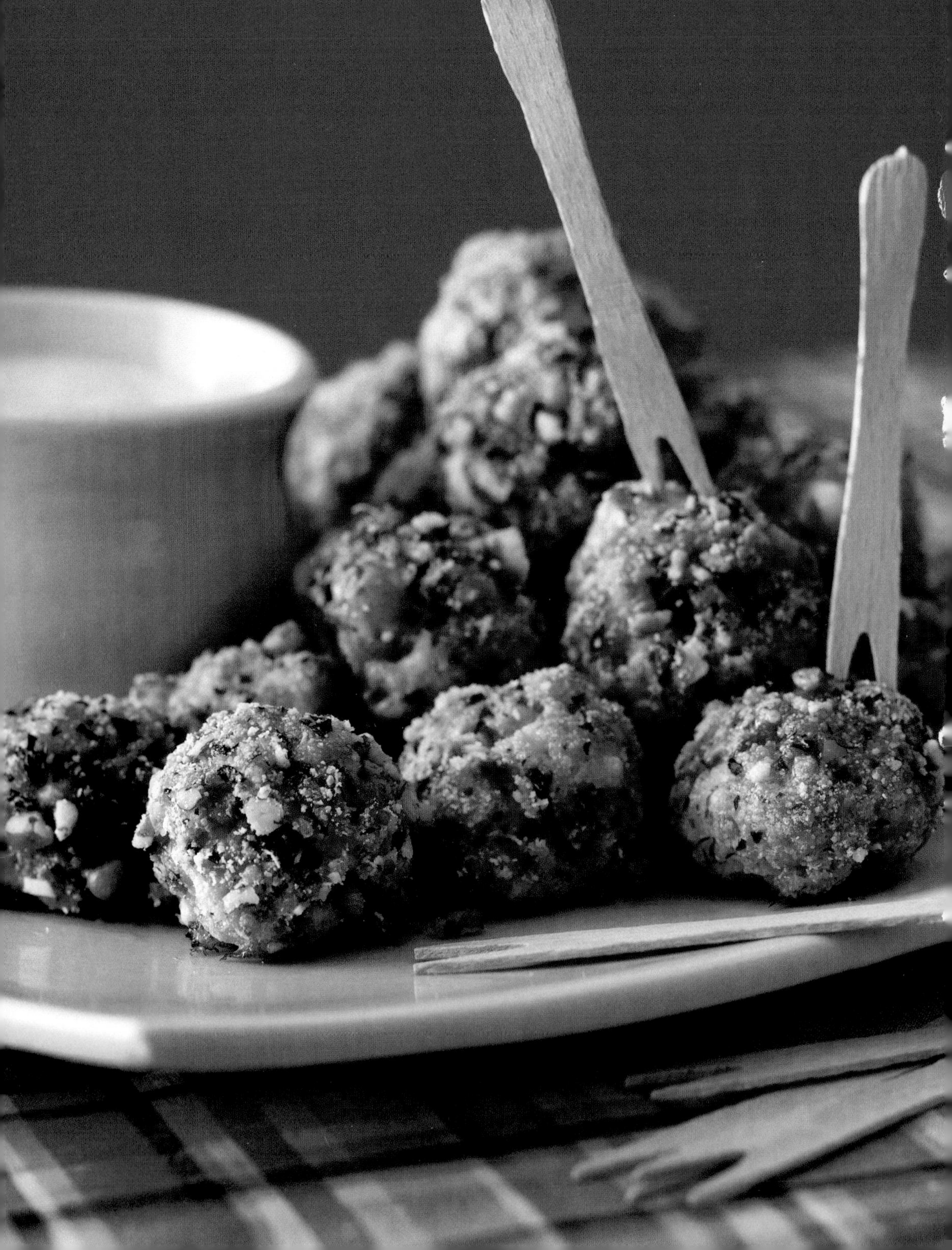

Spicy Party Meatballs with Mango-Yogurt Sauce

Gail Seymour, Nederland, TX

Gail and her family enjoy all kinds of meatballs, so she cleverly came up with these chicken and sausage balls to fit the Weight Watchers profile. In a stroke of culinary genius, she teamed them with a unique and refreshing tropical mango-yogurt sauce.

MEATBALLS

- ½ pound ground skinless chicken breast
- 6 ounces sweet Italian turkey sausage, casings removed
- ½ cup + 3 tablespoons plain dry bread crumbs
- ½ green bell pepper, minced
- ¼ cup fat-free cottage cheese
- 2 egg whites, lightly beaten
- 2 scallions, thinly sliced
- 1 tablespoon Worcestershire sauce
- 3 tablespoons grated Parmesan cheese
- 1 tablespoon chopped pecans

MANGO SAUCE

- 1 mango, peeled and cubed
- ¾ cup fat-free plain yogurt
- ¼ cup fat-free half-and-half
- 1 tablespoon orange juice
- 1 tablespoon honey
- ½ teaspoon ground pepper

MAKES 15 SERVINGS

1. Preheat the oven to 400°F. Spray a nonstick 10 x 15-inch jelly-roll pan with nonstick spray.

2. To make the meatballs, combine the chicken, sausage, ½ cup of the bread crumbs, the bell pepper, cottage cheese, egg whites, scallions, and Worcestershire sauce in a large bowl. Shape into 30 (1-inch) balls.

3. Place the Parmesan cheese, pecans, and the remaining 3 tablespoons bread crumbs on wax paper. Roll the balls in the cheese mixture to coat evenly. Place in a single layer without touching each other on the jelly-roll pan. Bake until cooked through and lightly browned, about 25 minutes.

4. Meanwhile, to make the sauce, pulse the mango, yogurt, half-and-half, orange juice, honey, and pepper in a food processor until smooth. Serve with the meatballs.

PER SERVING (2 meatballs with 2 tablespoons sauce): 88 Cal, 2 g Fat, 1 g Sat Fat, 0 g Trans Fat, 16 mg Chol, 184 mg Sod, 10 g Carb, 1 g Fib, 8 g Prot, 64 mg Calc. *POINTS* value: *2*.

tip For an elegant presentation, place a bowl of the sauce on a platter lined with watercress. Skewer the meatballs on party picks and place on the watercress.

Stuffed Grape Leaves

Mary Guleserian, Orange, CA

"This has been a requested dish at family gatherings," Mary writes. "The recipe has changed over the years. My mother used ground lamb, but as we became more fat conscious, I switched to lean ground turkey and not one of my relatives noticed!"

1 (8-ounce) jar grape leaves, rinsed, drained, and patted dry with paper towels

1 pound ground skinless turkey breast

¾ cup long-grain white rice

½ cup finely chopped onion

2 garlic cloves, minced

2 tablespoons chopped fresh mint

½ teaspoon salt

½ teaspoon freshly ground pepper

1 (8-ounce) can tomato sauce

1 cup cold water

1 tablespoon fresh lemon juice

MAKES 12 SERVINGS

1. Spray a large nonstick Dutch oven with nonstick spray. Sort the grape leaves and spread any ripped ones on the bottom of the pot. Save 24 whole leaves for stuffing.

2. Combine the turkey, rice, onion, garlic, mint, salt, and pepper in a large bowl. Trim any tough stems from the grape leaves. Working with one leaf at a time, place 1 rounded tablespoon of the filling in the center of the bottom third of the leaf. Fold over the sides then roll up from the bottom to form a package. Place the roll, seam-side down, in the Dutch oven. Repeat with remaining grape leaves and filling to make 24 stuffed grape leaves.

3. Combine the tomato sauce, water, and lemon juice in a medium bowl. Pour the sauce over the grape leaves in the Dutch oven. Place a heatproof plate directly on top of the leaves to prevent them from opening. Cover the pot, and bring to a boil. Reduce the heat and simmer, until the grape leaves are tender and the rice is cooked, about 1 hour. Transfer the grape leaves to a serving platter and top with the sauce.

PER SERVING (2 stuffed grape leaves with 2 tablespoons sauce): 99 Cal, 1 g Fat, 0 g Sat Fat, 0 g Trans Fat, 25 mg Chol, 364 mg Sod, 13 g Carb, 1 g Fib, 11 g Prot, 41 mg Calc. *POINTS* value: 2.

Salmon Nuggets

Patricia SeCoy, Redding, CA

Patricia, who has lost over 11 pounds so far on the program, makes this dish in the summer after she's been fishing. For an elegant presentation, thread three salmon pieces on each of eight mini bamboo skewers, arrange on small black-lacquered trays, and garnish with scallion flowers (see tip).

1 tablespoon reduced-sodium
  soy sauce
1 tablespoon mirin or other
  rice wine
1 teaspoon cornstarch
2 teaspoons minced peeled
  fresh ginger
1 garlic clove, minced
1 (1-pound) salmon fillet, cut
  into 24 (1-inch-thick) pieces
1 teaspoon peanut oil
2 scallions, thinly sliced
  diagonally

MAKES 8 SERVINGS

1. Combine the soy sauce, mirin, cornstarch, ginger, and garlic in a medium bowl. Add the salmon; toss to coat. Refrigerate, covered, at least 1 hour.

2. Heat the oil in a large nonstick skillet over medium-high heat. Add the salmon in one layer and cook, turning occasionally, until golden on the outside and opaque in the center, about 4 minutes. Place a toothpick in each piece of salmon, arrange on a plate, and sprinkle with the scallions.

PER SERVING (3 pieces): 85 Cal, 3 g Fat, 0 g Sat Fat, 0 g Trans Fat, 32 mg Chol, 118 mg Sod, 1 g Carb, 0 g Fib, 13 g Prot, 11 mg Calc. *POINTS* value: 2.

tip To make decorative scallion flowers for a pretty garnish, cut away all but 2 to 3 inches of the green part attached to the bulb of the scallion; trim the roots from the bulb. With a sharp pointed knife, make $1/2$-inch long, thin slits into the bulb and into the green end. Place in iced water until the ends fan open, about 10 minutes.

COCONUT SHRIMP

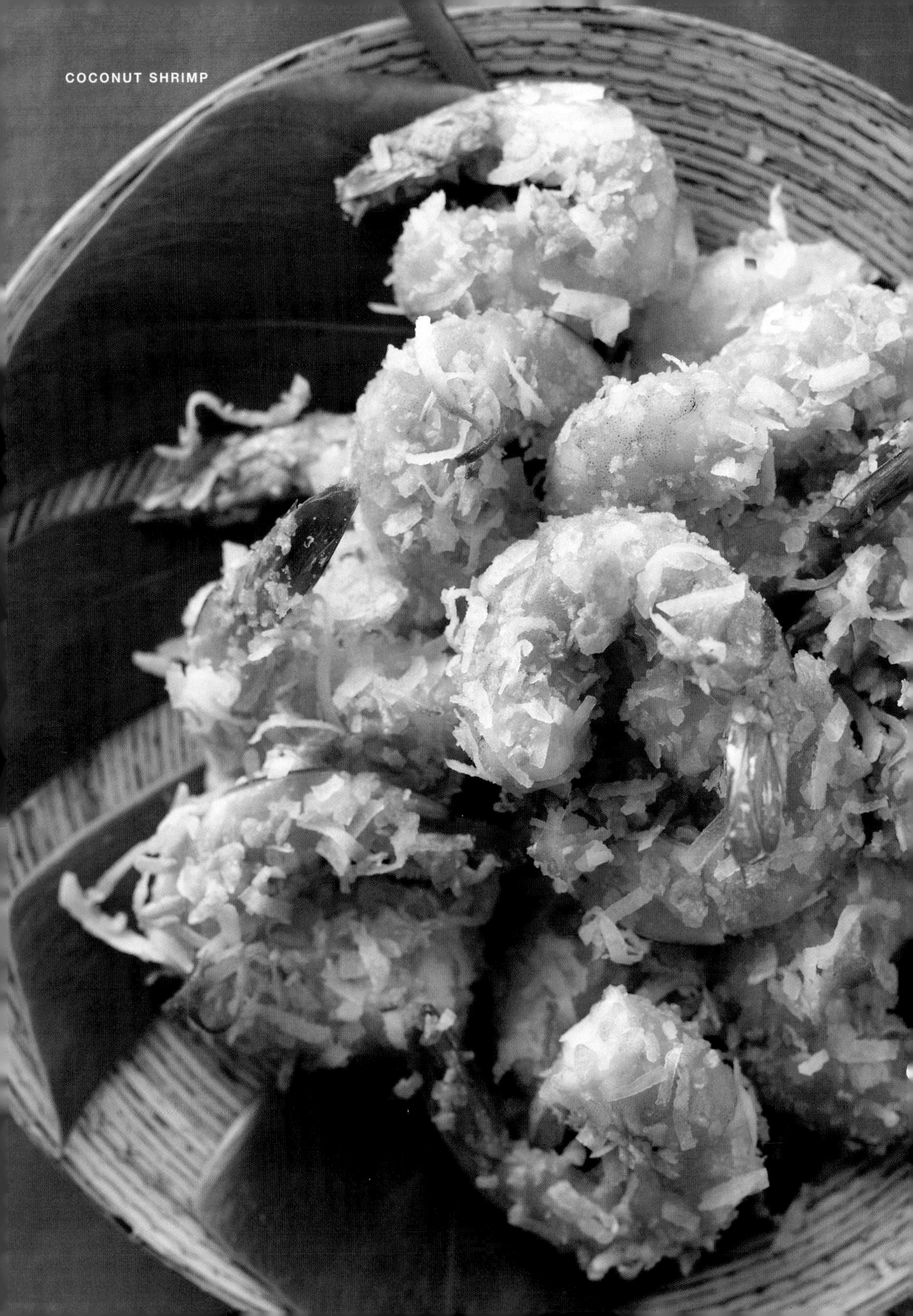

Coconut Shrimp

Glenna L. Ryan, Schenectady, NY

Glenna loves coconut shrimp and was inspired to create this healthy, low-fat version for her family for special occasions. The cornflake-coconut coating gives it a crunchy texture the whole family loves. Concerning her weight-loss journey she writes, "It's a daily challenge, but I want my two little girls to have a good role model." For a sweet complement, serve the shrimp with mango chutney (2 tablespoons will increase your *POINTS* value by 1) or apricot preserves (1 tablespoon will increase your *POINTS* value by 1).

¼ cup fat-free milk

3 tablespoons all-purpose flour

24 (about ½ pound) medium
shrimp, peeled and deveined,
tails left on

½ cup flaked coconut, chopped

¼ cup cornflake crumbs

MAKES 8 SERVINGS

1. Preheat the oven to 450°F. Spray a 10 x 15-inch jelly-roll pan with nonstick spray.

2. Whisk together the milk and flour in a large bowl. Add the shrimp; toss to coat.

3. Place the coconut and cornflake crumbs in a large zip-close plastic bag. Add the shrimp, a few pieces at a time, and shake to coat. Place the shrimp in the jelly-roll pan in one layer. Lightly spray with nonstick spray. Bake until the shrimp are golden on the outside and opaque in the center, about 5 minutes on each side.

PER SERVING (3 shrimp): 75 Cal, 3 g Fat, 3 g Sat Fat, 0 g Trans Fat, 32 mg Chol, 84 mg Sod, 8 g Carb, 1 g Fib, 5 g Prot, 16 mg Calc. **POINTS** value: **2**.

tip If you can't find cornflake crumbs, you can make your own by placing regular cornflakes in a zip-close plastic bag then finely crush them with a rolling pin. Spray the knife with nonstick spray to keep the coconut from sticking as you chop.

APPETIZERS

Baked Clams Oreganata

Linda Cavallaro, Poughkeepsie, NY

"This was my grandmother's favorite recipe—and a favorite at our house on Christmas Eve," writes Linda, who has lost 53 pounds on the Weight Watchers program. If you're not comfortable opening clams yourself, have the fishmonger open them, reserving the juice and shells. If you like, substitute a 6½-ounce can of chopped clams in place of the fresh clams. Simply drain the clams, stir into the bread crumb mixture, spoon into twelve (4-inch) ovenproof ramekin dishes, then follow the directions from step 3.

⅔ cup seasoned dry bread crumbs

2 tablespoons chopped fresh parsley

1 teaspoon grated lemon zest

½ teaspoon dried oregano

1 garlic clove, minced

3 drops hot pepper sauce

12 cherrystone clams, scrubbed and shucked (12 half-shells and ⅓ cup of clam juice reserved)

2 tablespoons fresh lemon juice

2 tablespoons reduced-calorie margarine, melted

6 lemon wedges

MAKES 6 SERVINGS

1. Combine the bread crumbs, parsley, lemon zest, oregano, garlic, and hot pepper sauce in a medium bowl, rubbing with fingertips to infuse the crumbs with flavor. Stir in the reserved clam juice (mixture should be crumbly).

2. Preheat the broiler. Arrange the 12 clam half-shells on a broiler pan or jelly-roll pan. Place a clam in each shell and top with the crumb mixture.

3. Combine the lemon juice and melted margarine in a small bowl. Drizzle 1 teaspoon lemon mixture over each clam. Broil 6 inches from the heat until the crumbs are golden and clams are just cooked through, 8–9 minutes. Serve with the lemon wedges.

PER SERVING (2 clams): 103 Cal, 4 g Fat, 1 g Sat Fat, 0 g Trans Fat, 8 mg Chol, 428 mg Sod, 12 g Carb, 1 g Fib, 5 g Prot, 33 mg Calc. *POINTS* value: *2.*

Crab Spread

Bernice Landry, Atholville, New Brunswick, Canada

Bernice finds her Weight Watchers meetings "fun, interesting, and very important," and has lost 19 pounds on the program. Since crabmeat is so readily available in her area, this is one of her favorite things to serve for social gatherings and potlucks. You can serve this with your favorite fat-free crackers or baked tortilla chips.

1¼ cups fat-free cottage cheese

3 ounces fat-free cream cheese, at room temperature

1 pound cooked lump crabmeat, picked over and flaked

½ cup shredded reduced-fat cheddar cheese

2 scallions, chopped

1 tablespoon fresh lemon juice

1 teaspoon Worcestershire sauce

1 teaspoon mustard powder

¼ teaspoon salt

3–4 drops hot pepper sauce

MAKES 14 SERVINGS

1. Preheat the oven to 375°F. Spray a 1-quart baking dish with nonstick spray.

2. Beat the cottage cheese and cream cheese with an electric mixer on medium speed in a large bowl until smooth and creamy. Stir in the crab, cheddar cheese, scallions, lemon juice, Worcestershire sauce, mustard, salt, and hot pepper sauce. Transfer to the baking dish.

3. Bake, uncovered, until bubbly, about 25 minutes. Serve hot or let cool slightly and serve warm.

PER SERVING (¼ cup): 78 Cal, 3 g Fat, 1 g Sat Fat, 0 g Trans Fat, 34 mg Chol, 290 mg Sod, 2 g Carb, 0 g Fib, 10 g Prot, 82 mg Calc. *POINTS* value: 2.

tip Lump crabmeat is available fresh or frozen and can be quite expensive. A 1-pound can of crabmeat, or imitation crab, is less expensive and can be substituted here if you like. Be sure to carefully pick through all crabmeat—fresh, frozen, or canned—to remove any shell or cartilage.

ASIAN PHYLLO ROLLS
WITH HONEY-APRICOT
DIPPING SAUCE

Asian Phyllo Rolls with Honey-Apricot Dipping Sauce

Julie DeMatteo, Clementon, NJ

Julie first created these delicious rolls for friends and family who came to her house for Super Bowl Sunday. "They absolutely raved about them," she writes.

½ cup apricot preserves

3 tablespoons seasoned rice vinegar

1 tablespoon honey

4 teaspoons minced peeled fresh ginger

2 garlic cloves, minced

2 teaspoons Asian (dark) sesame oil

¼ teaspoon crushed red pepper

2 teaspoons canola oil

½ pound ground skinless turkey breast

2 cups frozen Asian-style vegetables, thawed, patted dry, and chopped

1 cup chopped bok choy

2 tablespoons reduced-sodium soy sauce

2 tablespoons water

1 teaspoon sugar

8 (12 x 17-inch) sheets phyllo dough, thawed according to package directions

MAKES 8 SERVINGS

1. To make the sauce, combine the preserves, vinegar, honey, 2 teaspoons of the ginger, the garlic, 1 teaspoon of the sesame oil, and the crushed red pepper in a bowl. Cover and refrigerate.

2. To make rolls, heat canola oil in a large nonstick skillet over medium-high heat. Add turkey and brown, about 6 minutes. Add vegetables and bok choy. Cook, stirring until tender, about 4 minutes. Stir in soy sauce, water, remaining 2 teaspoons ginger and 1 teaspoon sesame oil, and the sugar. Cook 5 minutes. Let cool.

3. Preheat the oven to 400°F. Spray a large baking sheet with nonstick spray. Place one sheet of phyllo with the short side facing you on a work surface. Lightly spray the phyllo sheet with nonstick spray. Then fold it in half lengthwise. Place ½ cup of the filling in the center of the bottom end of the phyllo. Fold in the sides then roll up to completely enclose the filling. Place the roll, seam-side down, on the baking sheet. Lightly spray the roll with nonstick spray. Repeat with remaining phyllo and filling to make 8 rolls. Bake until light golden, 15–20 minutes. Serve with the dipping sauce.

PER SERVING (1 roll with 2 tablespoons dipping sauce): 168 Cal, 4 g Fat, 1 g Sat Fat, 0 g Trans Fat, 19 mg Chol, 380 mg Sod, 25 g Carb, 1 g Fib, 9 g Prot, 24 mg Calc. *POINTS* value: **3**.

Spring Rolls

Cynthia Brown, Portland, OR

"I was looking for a way for my family to eat cruciferous vegetables, such as cabbage and broccoli, without knowing it," says Cynthia. Since they all love Chinese food, she cleverly adjusted a regular spring roll recipe to cut the fat and incorporate packaged coleslaw and broccoli slaw—and so this family favorite was born! It is easily made in under 30 minutes. If you can't find broccoli slaw, use the entire bag of coleslaw.

2 teaspoons peanut oil

½ (1-pound) package coleslaw

½ (1-pound) package broccoli slaw, coarsely chopped

1 tablespoon reduced-sodium soy sauce

1 teaspoon chili-garlic sauce or ½ teaspoon crushed red pepper

½ teaspoon Asian (dark) sesame oil

½ teaspoon sugar

8 (6-inch square) egg roll wrappers

MAKES 8 SERVINGS

1. Heat the oil in a large nonstick skillet over medium-high heat. Add the coleslaw and the broccoli slaw and cook, stirring frequently, over medium-high heat, until softened, about 4 minutes. If the mixture seems too dry, add a little water. Add the soy sauce, chili sauce, sesame oil, and sugar. Cook over medium heat until the flavors are blended, about 3 minutes longer. Set aside to cool slightly.

2. Preheat the oven to 350°F. Spray a large baking sheet with nonstick spray; set aside.

3. Lightly moisten the edges of one egg roll wrapper with water. Place a scant ¼ cup of the filling in the center. Fold in the sides then roll up to completely enclose the filling. Place the roll, seam-side down, on the baking sheet. Lightly spray the roll with nonstick spray. Repeat with the remaining egg roll wrappers, filling, and nonstick spray to make 8 rolls. Bake the rolls until light golden, 20–25 minutes. Serve hot.

PER SERVING (1 egg roll): 111 Cal, 2 g Fat, 0 g Sat Fat, 0 g Trans Fat, 3 mg Chol, 273 mg Sod, 20 g Carb, 2 g Fib, 4 g Prot, 39 mg Calc. *POINTS* value: *2.*

Baked Stuffed Wontons

Janet Granai-Benway, Burlington, VT

Janet, now a Lifetime member, joined Weight Watchers with her husband Gary, who "had to eat these wontons for many weekends until I perfected this recipe," she writes. "Never once did he complain!" These mini delights are great party finger food. If you like, substitute shredded cabbage for the salad greens.

1 teaspoon canola oil

½ onion, finely chopped

½ red bell pepper, seeded and diced

1 (4½-ounce) can chopped mild green chiles

1 cup mixed salad greens, chopped

½ teaspoon salt

½ cup shredded reduced-fat cheddar cheese

24 (3½-inch square) wonton wrappers

½ cup canned mixed vegetable juice or tomato juice

2 tablespoons chopped fresh cilantro

2 tablespoons chopped scallions

3 drops hot pepper sauce

MAKES 12 SERVINGS

1. Heat the oil in a medium nonstick skillet over medium heat. Add the onion and bell pepper and cook, stirring frequently, until softened, about 8 minutes. Stir in the chiles, salad greens, and salt and cook, stirring frequently, until the salad greens are just wilted, about 3 minutes. Remove from heat and stir in cheese; cool slightly.

2. Preheat the oven to 350°F. Spray two 12-cup mini-muffin tins with nonstick spray. Press 1 wonton wrapper into each cup; lightly spray with nonstick spray. Bake until golden, about 5 minutes. Remove tins from oven. Leave oven on.

3. Remove wrappers from tins and transfer to a large baking sheet. Place 2 teaspoons of the vegetable mixture in the center of each wrapper. Spray lightly with nonstick spray. Bake until golden and crisp, about 10 minutes.

4. Meanwhile, to prepare the sauce, combine vegetable juice, cilantro, scallions, and hot pepper sauce in small bowl. Serve with the wontons.

PER SERVING (2 wontons with 1 tablespoon dipping sauce): 72 Cal, 2 g Fat, 1 g Sat Fat, 0 g Trans Fat, 5 mg Chol, 256 mg Sod, 11 g Carb, 1 g Fib, 3 g Prot, 62 mg Calc. *POINTS* value: *1.*

Crab Rangoon

Pat Shepich, Troy, MI

Lifetime member and retired teacher Pat writes, "I served this at my book discussion group and didn't tell them it was low-fat or low-*POINTS* value (four of us are Weight Watchers members). They loved it! So I told them." This popular Chinese appetizer is typically made with creamy crab filling and deep-fried. Pat's trimmer version uses economical imitation crabmeat and the wontons are baked, instead of deep-fried.

1 (8-ounce) package imitation crabmeat

1 (8-ounce) package fat-free cream cheese, at room temperature

1 teaspoon bottled steak sauce

1 garlic clove, minced

24 (3½-inch square) wonton wrappers

MAKES 12 SERVINGS

1. Preheat the oven to 375°F. Spray a nonstick baking sheet with nonstick spray.

2. Combine the crabmeat, cream cheese, steak sauce, and garlic in a medium bowl until blended.

3. Arrange 6 of the wonton wrappers on a work surface. Place 1 tablespoon of the crab mixture in the center of each wrapper. Brush the edges of each wonton wrapper with water then fold into triangles, pressing the edges to seal. Place the filled wontons on the baking sheet. Repeat with the remaining wrappers and filling, making a total of 24 wontons. Spray the wontons lightly with nonstick spray.

4. Bake until the wontons are golden and crisp, about 20 minutes. Serve hot.

PER SERVING (2 pieces): 85 Cal, 1 g Fat, 0 g Sat Fat, 0 g Trans Fat, 7 mg Chol, 358 mg Sod, 13 g Carb, 0 g Fib, 7 g Prot, 45 mg Calc. **POINTS** value: 2.

tip For a change of pace, you can add chopped scallions and a little minced, peeled fresh ginger to the filling.

APPETIZERS

Spinach Tartlets

Melodi Choate, Chicago, IL

Pretty enough for any buffet table, these tasty little treats filled with spinach, garlic, and cheese can be put together and served in under 20 minutes. Melodi likes to bring them to family gatherings.

1 (2.1-ounce, 15-shell) package frozen, fully baked mini phyllo dough shells

1 teaspoon extra-virgin olive oil

1 (10-ounce) package frozen chopped spinach, thawed and squeezed dry

2 garlic cloves, minced

⅓ cup crumbled reduced-fat feta cheese

MAKES 5 SERVINGS

1. Preheat the oven to 350°F. Arrange the phyllo shells in one layer on a 10 x 15-inch jelly-roll pan; set aside.

2. Heat the oil in a medium nonstick skillet over medium-high heat. Add the spinach and garlic and cook, stirring frequently, until softened, about 3 minutes. Remove from the heat. Stir in the cheese. Spoon about 2 teaspoons of the spinach mixture into each shell.

3. Bake until the filling is hot and the tops are lightly browned, about 10 minutes.

PER SERVING (3 pieces): 104 Cal, 5 g Fat, 1 g Sat Fat, 0 g Trans Fat, 3 mg Chol, 170 mg Sod, 10 g Carb, 2 g Fib, 5 g Prot, 78 mg Calc. *POINTS* value: 2.

tip Make sure to thoroughly squeeze the spinach so it is completely dry. The best way to do this is to drain it through a sieve then use both hands to squeeze out the excess liquid.

Mushroom Strudel

Julie S. Ely Feeding Hills, MA

"I travel constantly and find the **POINTS** value program allows me the flexibility I need," says Weight Watchers member, Julie.

2 teaspoons butter

1 (8-ounce) package fresh
   mushrooms, thinly sliced

1 shallot, finely chopped

¼ teaspoon salt

¼ cup fat-free cream cheese,
   at room temperature

1 teaspoon chopped
   fresh thyme

3 (12 x 17-inch) sheets phyllo
   dough, thawed according to
   package directions

MAKES 4 SERVINGS

1. Preheat the oven to 375°F. Spray a baking sheet with nonstick spray.

2. Melt the butter in a medium nonstick skillet over medium-high heat. Add the mushrooms, shallot, and salt. Cook, stirring frequently, until the mushrooms are tender and any liquid has evaporated, about 8 minutes. Stir in the cream cheese and thyme. Set aside to cool.

3. Place one sheet of the phyllo with the short side facing you on a work surface (cover remaining phyllo with plastic wrap to retain moisture). Lightly spray the phyllo sheet with nonstick spray; top with a second phyllo sheet and lightly spray with nonstick spray. Repeat with the remaining phyllo sheet and nonstick spray. Fold the sheets crosswise in half. Spread the mushroom filling along the bottom, leaving a 1-inch margin at the edges. Fold in the sides then roll up to completely enclose the filling. Place the roll, seam-side down, on the baking sheet. Lightly spray the roll with nonstick spray.

4. Bake until the phyllo is golden, about 20 minutes. Cool on a rack about 10 minutes. Cut the strudel into 8 pieces and serve warm.

PER SERVING (2 pieces): 91 Cal, 3 g Fat, 2 g Sat Fat, 0 g Trans Fat, 6 mg Chol, 296 mg Sod, 12 g Carb, 1 g Fib, 5 g Prot, 35 mg Calc. **POINTS** value: 2.

MUSHROOM STRUDEL

Spinach, Artichoke, and Ricotta Bites

Crystal Ralph-Haughn, Bartlesville, OK

"I love the dishes at restaurants that feature spinach and artichokes," says Crystal, who used her two favorite ingredients as the basis for these delicious treats.

1 (8-ounce) tube refrigerated, reduced-fat crescent dinner roll dough

1 (14-ounce) can artichoke hearts, rinsed, drained, and coarsely chopped

1 (10-ounce) package frozen chopped spinach, thawed and squeezed dry

1 cup part-skim ricotta cheese

¼ cup oil-packed sun-dried tomatoes, drained, patted dry with paper towels, and chopped

¼ cup grated Parmesan cheese

½ teaspoon freshly ground pepper

16 cherry tomatoes, each sliced into thirds

MAKES 16 SERVINGS

1. Preheat the oven to 375°F. Separate the dough to make 4 rectangles and arrange them on an ungreased nonstick 10 x 15-inch jelly-roll pan. Using your fingers, press the dough to the edges of the pan to make a crust. Bake until light golden, 10–12 minutes. Remove the pan from the oven. Leave the oven on.

2. Meanwhile, combine the artichoke hearts, spinach, ricotta cheese, sun-dried tomatoes, and 2 tablespoons of the Parmesan cheese in a large bowl. Spread filling over the baked crust. Top evenly with remaining 2 tablespoons Parmesan cheese and the pepper. Bake until the bottom is browned and the filling is hot, about 15 minutes. Cut into 48 (1½-inch) squares then top each square with a cherry tomato slice.

PER SERVING (3 squares): 96 Cal, 4 g Fat, 2 g Sat Fat, 0 g Trans Fat, 6 mg Chol, 215 mg Sod, 10 g Carb, 1 g Fib, 4 g Prot, 73 mg Calc. *POINTS* value: 2.

Quiche Squares

Donna Childs, New York, NY

"Tasty and low in calories, you can enjoy these quiche squares and not feel deprived," says Donna. She serves them as "party food" or as a "main course for dinner sometimes." We think salsa is a good condiment to serve with them—you might like to try one of the salsas in this chapter.

1 cup fat-free cottage cheese

½ cup shredded reduced-fat
    Monterey Jack cheese

1 (4½-ounce) can chopped
    mild green chiles

6 tablespoons all-purpose flour

¾ teaspoon baking powder

2 large eggs, lightly beaten

1 egg white, lightly beaten

¼ teaspoon salt

MAKES 8 SERVINGS

1. Preheat the oven to 350°F. Spray an 8-inch-square baking pan with nonstick spray.

2. Combine the cottage cheese, Monterey Jack cheese, chiles, flour, baking powder, eggs, egg white, and salt in a large bowl until well blended. Scrape the mixture into the pan. Bake until the top is golden and a knife inserted in the center comes out clean, about 30 minutes. Cut into 16 squares and serve at once. Or cool completely in the pan on a rack then cut into 16 squares and serve at room temperature.

PER SERVING (2 pieces): 85 Cal, 3 g Fat, 1 g Sat Fat, 0 g Trans Fat, 59 mg Chol, 360 mg Sod, 7 g Carb, 1 g Fib, 8 g Prot, 106 mg Calc. **POINTS** value: *2.*

tip For a light lunch or dinner, bake in a 9-inch round pie plate and cut into wedges.

APPETIZERS

Basil and Olive–Stuffed Mushrooms

Lori McWilliams-Gersbach, Philadelphia, PA

Lifetime member Lori created these delicious mushrooms when a friend gave her a bunch of fragrant fresh basil. We often say you can substitute dried herbs for fresh, at the ratio of 1 tablespoon fresh to 1 teaspoon dried. In this recipe we don't recommend substituting dried basil for fresh—it just doesn't cut it. If you can't find fresh basil, use chopped flat-leaf parsley instead.

⅔ cup plain dry bread crumbs

¼ cup chopped fresh basil

5 oil-cured black olives, pitted and chopped (about 1 tablespoon)

1 tablespoon grated Parmesan cheese

1 tablespoon low-sodium chicken broth or dry white wine

1 tablespoon olive oil

12 fresh white mushrooms (about ½ pound), stems discarded

MAKES 6 SERVINGS

1. Preheat the oven to 400°F. Spray a nonstick 10 x 15-inch jelly-roll pan with nonstick spray.

2. Combine the bread crumbs, basil, olives, cheese, broth, and oil in a medium bowl.

3. Place the mushroom caps on the jelly-roll pan. Fill the cavity of each mushroom with the crumb mixture, mounding it slightly. Lightly spray with nonstick spray. Bake until the mushrooms are tender and the crumbs are browned, about 25 minutes. Serve hot.

PER SERVING (2 stuffed mushrooms): 90 Cal, 4 g Fat, 1 g Sat Fat, 0 g Trans Fat, 1 mg Chol, 178 mg Sod, 11 g Carb, 1 g Fib, 3 g Prot, 45 mg Calc. *POINTS* value: 2.

Stuffed Portobello Mushrooms

Cynthia Johnson, Bellingham, WA

Cynthia is committed to becoming a Lifetime member, and with a 10-pound weight loss so far, she is on her way to reaching that goal. She sometimes serves these delicious mushrooms, with wonderful Mediterranean flavors, for a quick lunch with a green salad on the side.

¼ (14-ounce) can artichoke hearts, rinsed, drained, and finely chopped (about 2 artichoke hearts)

1 plum tomato, seeded and chopped

2 tablespoons plain dry bread crumbs

1 tablespoon reduced-fat feta cheese, crumbled

1 tablespoon chopped fresh parsley

4 kalamata olives, pitted and chopped

2 teaspoons extra-virgin olive oil

2 large Portobello mushrooms (about ½ pound), stems discarded, caps wiped clean

MAKES 4 SERVINGS

1. Preheat the oven to 425°F. Spray a nonstick 10 x 15-inch jelly-roll pan with nonstick spray.

2. Combine the artichoke hearts, tomato, bread crumbs, cheese, parsley, olives, and oil in a small bowl.

3. Place the mushroom caps on the jelly-roll pan. Fill the cavity of each mushroom with the artichoke mixture, mounding it slightly. Lightly spray with nonstick spray. Bake until the mushrooms are tender and the filling is hot, about 20 minutes. Cut each mushroom into four wedges. Serve hot.

PER SERVING (2 wedges): 97 Cal, 4 g Fat, 1 g Sat Fat, 0 g Trans Fat, 1 mg Chol, 224 mg Sod, 10 g Carb, 1 g Fib, 4 g Prot, 14 mg Calc. *POINTS* value: 2.

tip Portobello mushrooms vary in size, but for this recipe you'll need them about 4 inches in diameter. To make ahead, stuff the mushrooms (but don't bake them) then cover and refrigerate overnight. When ready to serve, bake in a 400°F oven until heated through, about 25 minutes.

APPETIZERS

Bistro Breaded Vegetables

Tammy Hard, Quincy, MI

Who says breaded veggies have to be deep-fried to taste good? Tammy's baked version is so delicious you'll never miss the oil, and certainly not the fat and calories. "I know my Weight Watchers recipes are a hit with the family when they start requesting them," says Tammy. "My seven-year-old, Erin, asked if we could have them on her birthday."

½ cup fat-free milk

2 tablespoons light mayonnaise

1 egg white, lightly beaten

2 cups large cauliflower florets (about 12 pieces)

12 whole mushrooms, stems removed

1 medium zucchini, cut into 12 (½-inch-thick) slices

½ cup plain dry bread crumbs

¼ cup grated Parmesan cheese

1 teaspoon paprika

½ teaspoon dried tarragon

¼ teaspoon salt

¼ teaspoon freshly ground pepper

MAKES 12 SERVINGS

1. Preheat the oven to 400°F. Spray a large baking sheet with nonstick spray.

2. Combine the milk, mayonnaise, and egg white in a large bowl. Add the cauliflower, mushrooms, and zucchini; toss to coat.

3. Place the bread crumbs, cheese, paprika, tarragon, salt, and pepper in a zip-close plastic bag. Add the cauliflower, mushrooms, and zucchini, in batches, shaking the bag to coat all sides. Arrange the vegetables in one layer on the baking sheet. Spray the top of the vegetables lightly with nonstick spray. Bake, turning once halfway through cooking time, until the vegetables are tender and golden, about 30 minutes. Serve at once.

PER SERVING (3 pieces): 51 Cal, 2 g Fat, 1 g Sat Fat, 0 g Trans Fat, 2 mg Chol, 155 mg Sod, 6 g Carb, 1 g Fib, 3 g Prot, 54 mg Calc. *POINTS* value: *1*.

tip If you'd like to use fresh broccoli florets instead of the cauliflower florets, cook them in boiling water until tender crisp, about 3 minutes. Drain the broccoli and pat dry then proceed with steps 2 and 3.

Roasted Red Potato Bites

Karen Anderson-Gray, Aptos, CA

Karen belongs to a wine club, which requires her to bring an appetizer to each gathering. "Since I was counting my *POINTS*," she writes, "I wanted something which wouldn't blow my day's quota." She developed this tasty hors d'oeuvre, which—no surprise—"everyone at the wine club loved." If you can't find smoked Gouda cheese, smoked mozzarella is fine.

12 small whole new or red potatoes (about 1 pound), each cut in half

¼ cup smoked Gouda cheese, shredded

3 slices bacon, cooked and finely crumbled (about 2 tablespoons)

¼ cup fat-free sour cream

2 tablespoons chopped fresh chives

MAKES 12 SERVINGS

1. Preheat the oven to 400°F. Spray a nonstick 10 x 15-inch jelly-roll pan with nonstick spray.

2. With a spoon or a melon baller, make a ½-inch deep well in the top of each potato half.

3. Arrange the potatoes in a single layer on the baking sheet. Lightly spray the potatoes with nonstick spray. Bake until tender and golden, about 40 minutes. Remove the potatoes from the oven. Leave the oven on.

4. Top each potato half with ½ teaspoon of the cheese and ¼ teaspoon of the bacon. Bake until the cheese begins to melt, about 5 minutes. Top each potato half with ½ teaspoon of the sour cream and sprinkle with the chives.

PER SERVING (2 pieces): 48 Cal, 2 g Fat, 1 g Sat Fat, 0 g Trans Fat, 5 mg Chol, 50 mg Sod, 6 g Carb, 1 g Fib, 2 g Prot, 25 mg Calc. *POINTS* value: **1.**

tip To help the potatoes stand flat on the baking tray, cut a small slice from the bottom of each potato half. If you don't have a melon baller, scoop out the potato flesh with a ¼ teaspoon measuring spoon.

APPETIZERS

Pizza Caponata

Linda E. Riederer, Hamburg, NY

Caponata, a flavorful Italian condiment made with eggplant, tomatoes, olives, and capers is usually served on little toasts or crackers. Here, Linda uses the convenience of prepared caponata and a prebaked pizza crust to put together this quick and easy appetizer.

1 tablespoon olive oil

1 (1-pound) eggplant, unpeeled and cut into ¾-inch chunks

1 (4¾-ounce) can caponata (eggplant condiment)

1 (1-pound) prebaked pizza crust

½ cup shredded part-skim mozzarella cheese

2 tablespoons grated Parmesan cheese

¼ cup chopped fresh basil

MAKES 12 SERVINGS

1. Preheat the oven to 450°F.

2. Heat the oil in a large nonstick skillet over medium heat. Add the eggplant and cook, stirring frequently, until tender and browned, about 8 minutes. Remove from the heat. Stir in the caponata.

3. Place the pizza crust on a baking sheet. Spread the eggplant mixture on the crust. Sprinkle evenly with the mozzarella cheese and Parmesan cheese. Bake until hot and the cheeses are lightly browned, 8–10 minutes.

4. To serve, slide the pizza onto a large cutting board, sprinkle with the basil then cut into 12 slices.

PER SERVING (1 slice): 151 Cal, 5 g Fat, 1 g Sat Fat, 0 g Trans Fat, 3 mg Chol, 291 mg Sod, 21 g Carb, 2 g Fib, 6 g Prot, 159 mg Calc. **POINTS** value: **3.**

Spinach and Salsa Pie

Lori Marie Moss, Westville, NJ

Lori's healthy, low-**POINTS** value appetizer is also great as an easy-to-prepare light lunch for two. The recipe is also easily doubled, baked in a 9 by 13-inch baking dish, and cut into squares.

1 (15-ounce) container fat-free ricotta cheese

1 (10-ounce) package frozen chopped spinach, thawed and squeezed dry

3 egg whites, lightly beaten

1 tablespoon cornstarch

¾ teaspoon salt

¼ teaspoon freshly ground pepper

¾ cup prepared salsa

¼ cup shredded reduced-fat sharp cheddar cheese

MAKES 8 SERVINGS

1. Preheat the oven to 375°F. Spray a 9-inch pie plate with nonstick spray.

2. Combine the ricotta cheese, spinach, egg whites, cornstarch, salt, and pepper in a large bowl. Scrape the filling into the pie plate. Spread the salsa over the top and out to the edges. Bake until the filling is set, and a knife inserted in the center comes out clean, about 30 minutes. Sprinkle the pie evenly with the cheddar cheese. Bake until the cheese is melted, about 5 minutes longer. Let stand 10 minutes before cutting into 8 slices.

PER SERVING (1 slice): 78 Cal, 1 g Fat, 1 g Sat Fat, 0 g Trans Fat, 11 mg Chol, 426 mg Sod, 8 g Carb, 2 g Fib, 8 g Prot, 159 mg Calc. **POINTS** value: **1**.

tip To thaw the spinach quickly, place it in a microwavable bowl and microwave on High for 2 minutes, stirring once, until thawed. Make sure to thoroughly squeeze the water from the spinach so it is completely dry.

CHAPTER 2

Soups and Salads

BOWLS OF COMFORT AND CRISPY GREENS

APPETIZERS

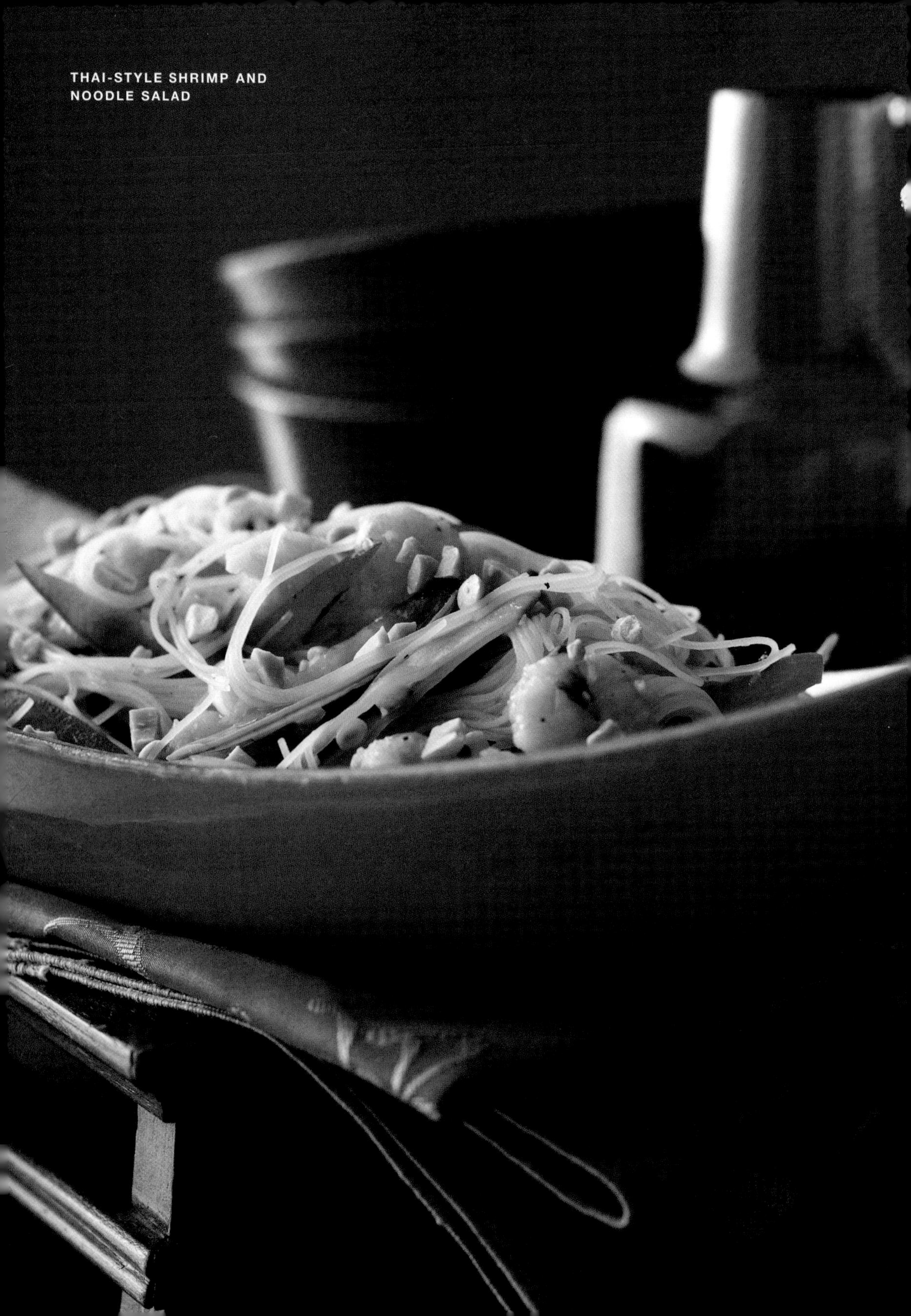

THAI-STYLE SHRIMP AND NOODLE SALAD

Thai-Style Shrimp and Noodle Salad

Linda Rohr, Westport, CT

Linda, who finds the Weight Watchers program "easy to follow," quickly reached her goal to lose 28 pounds and became a Lifetime member. She created this flavorful salad with a package of rice stick noodles she had on hand in her pantry and a few other ingredients from her refrigerator and freezer. Rice stick noodles are found in the ethnic section of most supermarkets. Since they involve no cooking, they couldn't be easier to prepare. Capellini (angel-hair pasta) is a good substitute— cook according to package directions.

¼ **pound rice stick noodles**

1 **(8-ounce) package frozen cooked salad shrimp, thawed**

1 **cup fresh snow peas, cut in half diagonally**

1 **red bell pepper, seeded and thinly sliced**

3 **scallions, thinly sliced**

¼ **cup chopped fresh cilantro**

½ **cup reduced-fat honey-Dijon dressing**

2 **tablespoons reduced-sodium soy sauce**

1 **tablespoon minced peeled fresh ginger**

2 **garlic cloves, minced**

2 **teaspoons Asian (dark) sesame oil**

¼ **teaspoon cayenne**

¼ **cup dry-roasted salted peanuts, chopped**

MAKES 6 SERVINGS

1. Place the noodles in a large bowl and add enough hot water to cover; let stand until soft, about 10 minutes; drain. Rinse under cold running water, about 1 minute; drain again. Place the noodles in a large bowl.

2. Add the shrimp, snow peas, bell pepper, scallions, and cilantro to the noodles.

3. Combine the dressing, soy sauce, ginger, garlic, oil, and cayenne in a small bowl; stir into the noodle and shrimp mixture. Sprinkle with the peanuts and serve at once.

PER SERVING (1 cup): 226 Cal, 8 g Fat, 1 g Sat Fat, 0 g Trans Fat, 74 mg Chol, 519 mg Sod, 26 g Carb, 2 g Fib, 13 g Prot, 44 mg Calc. **POINTS** value: 5.

tip To store leftover fresh ginger, peel and slice the root, then place in a jar with enough dry sherry or Madeira wine to cover. It will keep in the refrigerator for up to three months. The ginger and its liquid can be used in stir-fry dishes, salad dressings, and sauces.

SOUPS AND SALADS

Chipotle Sweet Potato Soup

Pam Dickson, Germantown, MD

Pam is a private chef for a group of people who belong to Weight Watchers. She inspires her clients because she has been successful on the program herself, losing 16 pounds and reaching her goal. Here is one of their favorite dishes—a delicious, velvety soup. The chipotle chiles and fresh ginger add bite and the sweet potatoes give just the right amount of sweetness.

1 tablespoon olive oil

1 onion, finely chopped

2 tablespoons packed light brown sugar

4 garlic cloves, minced

2 teaspoons minced peeled fresh ginger

1 chipotle en adobo, chopped

3 sweet potatoes (about 1½ pounds), peeled and cubed

6 cups low-sodium chicken broth

¾ cup dry white wine

¼ teaspoon salt

¼ teaspoon freshly ground pepper

1 (8-ounce) can fat-free evaporated milk

2 teaspoons grated lime zest

2 teaspoons fresh lime juice

Grated lime zest (optional)

MAKES 4 SERVINGS

1. Heat the oil in a large nonstick saucepan over medium-high heat. Add the onion and cook, stirring frequently, until tender, about 8 minutes. Add the sugar, garlic, ginger, and chipotle; cook, stirring constantly, until fragrant and blended, about 2 minutes.

2. Stir in the sweet potatoes, broth, wine, salt, and pepper; bring to a boil. Reduce the heat and simmer, stirring occasionally, until fork-tender, about 25 minutes.

3. Remove the pan from the heat; let the mixture cool for a few minutes. Transfer the mixture in batches to a food processor or blender and puree. Return the soup to the pan. Stir in the evaporated milk and return to a simmer. Remove from the heat and stir in the lime zest and juice. Serve each portion sprinkled with extra lime zest, if using.

PER SERVING (1½ cups): 208 Cal, 4 g Fat, 1 g Sat Fat, 0 g Trans Fat, 5 mg Chol, 405 mg Sod, 36 g Carb, 2 g Fib, 8 g Prot, 158 mg Calc. *POINTS* value: **4.**

tip If you want to make this soup vegetarian, use vegetable broth instead of chicken broth.

SOUPS AND SALADS

CHIPOTLE SWEET
POTATO SOUP

SOUTH-OF-THE-BORDER
CHICKEN SOUP

South-of-the-Border Chicken Soup

Carole Smith, Philadelphia, CA

Carole's festive and pretty Mexican soup, spiced with prepared salsa and a hint of cumin, cooks in less than 30 minutes! Kids and adults alike will love the crunchy tortilla and tasty cheese toppings.

1 teaspoon canola oil

½ pound skinless boneless chicken breast, cut into thin strips

1 onion, chopped

3 garlic cloves, minced

2 teaspoons ground cumin

4 cups low-sodium chicken broth

1 (14½-ounce) can diced tomatoes

1 (10-ounce) box frozen whole-kernel corn

1 cup prepared salsa

¼ cup chopped fresh cilantro

¼ cup shredded reduced-fat cheddar cheese

12 baked tortilla chips, crushed (about ½ cup)

MAKES 4 SERVINGS

1. Heat the oil in a large nonstick saucepan over medium-high heat. Add the chicken and cook until browned, about 6 minutes. Transfer the chicken to a plate; set aside.

2. Add the onion and garlic to the pan. Cook, stirring occasionally, until tender, about 8 minutes. Stir in the cumin and cook 1 minute. Add the broth, tomatoes, corn, and salsa; bring to a boil. Reduce the heat and simmer, uncovered, until the flavors are blended, about 10 minutes. Return the chicken to the pan; heat through. Remove the pan from the heat and stir in the cilantro. Serve the soup with the cheese and tortilla chips.

PER SERVING (2½ cups soup with 1 tablespoon cheese and 2 tablespoons crushed chips): 276 Cal, 7 g Fat, 3 g Sat Fat, 0 g Trans Fat, 41 mg Chol, 598 mg Sod, 36 g Carb, 7 g Fib, 22 g Prot, 152 mg Calc. *POINTS* value: 5.

My Thai Soup

Carol Fager-Higgens, San Francisco, CA

Carol writes, "I love Thai food, but the *POINTS* value is generally too high. My version of this soup cuts the *POINTS* value by using light coconut milk." Just be sure to use coconut milk, not its high-calorie counterpart, canned sweetened cream of coconut. Coconut milk, cilantro, ginger, chiles, and lemongrass are all staples in Thai cuisine and they add wonderful flavor to this exotic and satisfying soup.

2 teaspoons canola oil

1 (5-ounce) skinless boneless chicken breast, cut into thin strips

1 cup sliced fresh white mushrooms

1 red bell pepper, seeded and finely diced

1 tablespoon minced peeled fresh ginger

1 tablespoon finely chopped fresh lemongrass, or 1 teaspoon dried

1 small fresh red chile pepper, seeded and minced (wear gloves to prevent irritation)

2 cups low-sodium chicken broth

1 (14-ounce) can light coconut milk

2 teaspoons grated lime zest

2 teaspoons fresh lime juice

¼ cup chopped fresh cilantro

MAKES 4 SERVINGS

1. Heat the oil in a medium nonstick saucepan over medium-high heat. Add the chicken and cook, turning occasionally, until browned, about 4 minutes. Transfer the chicken to a plate; set aside.

2. Add the mushrooms and bell pepper to the pan. Cook over medium heat, stirring occasionally, until the vegetables are tender, about 6 minutes. Add the ginger, lemongrass, and chile pepper; cook, stirring constantly, until fragrant, about 1 minute.

3. Return the chicken to the pan. Add the broth, coconut milk, lime zest, and lime juice; bring to a boil. Reduce the heat and simmer, uncovered, until the flavors are blended, about 5 minutes. Stir in the cilantro and serve at once.

PER SERVING (generous 1 cup): 150 Cal, 9 g Fat, 4 g Sat Fat, 0 g Trans Fat, 21 mg Chol, 99 mg Sod, 9 g Carb, 2 g Fib, 10 g Prot, 20 mg Calc. *POINTS* value: 3.

tip Lemongrass is a fragrant lemony herb with long thin leaves and a bulbous base. To prepare, strip off and discard the outer fibrous leaves of the stalk then finely chop the white tender portion.

Grammy's Broccoli, Chicken, and Rice Soup

Edith Belobersycky, Calgary, Alberta, Canada

Edith has lost 32 pounds on Weight Watchers. She makes this healthy soup for her daughter's family on many a cold Canadian winter night. No doubt about it, grandmothers can teach us a thing or two—such as how to use leftovers to make a hearty, nutritious dinner and cook it all in one pot! You can use leftover turkey, beef, or pork instead of the chicken if you like.

2 teaspoons olive oil

1 cup chopped onions

1 cup sliced fresh white mushrooms

1 garlic clove, minced

1 tomato, seeded and chopped

6 cups low-sodium chicken broth

½ cup long-grain white rice

2 cups fresh broccoli florets

2 cups cubed cooked skinless chicken breast

¼ cup grated Parmesan cheese

½ teaspoon freshly ground pepper

MAKES 4 SERVINGS

1. Heat the oil in a large nonstick saucepan over medium-high heat. Add the onions, mushrooms, and garlic; cook, stirring often, until the vegetables are tender, about 8 minutes. Add the tomato and cook until soft, about 5 minutes.

2. Stir in the broth and rice; bring to a boil. Reduce the heat and simmer, covered, until the rice is tender, about 15 minutes. Stir in the broccoli and the chicken; return to a boil. Reduce the heat and simmer, partially covered, until the broccoli is tender and the chicken is heated through, about 5 minutes. Remove from the heat; stir in the cheese and pepper.

PER SERVING (2 cups): 336 Cal, 9 g Fat, 3 g Sat Fat, 0 g Trans Fat, 70 mg Chol, 322 mg Sod, 30 g Carb, 3 g Fib, 33 g Prot, 140 mg Calc. **POINTS** value: 7.

tip If you like, use a 10-ounce box of frozen broccoli spears thawed and coarsely chopped, instead of the fresh broccoli.

Chicken Gumbo

Rachel Reilly, Columbia, SC

Classic Creole cooking invariably contains a combination of chopped onion, celery, and green bell pepper, affectionately called "the trinity" by New Orleans chefs. It gives a good flavor base to many dishes such as this gumbo. A classic gumbo is traditionally thickened with a roux—a combination of cooked flour and butter—but Rachel has cleverly created a delicious, robust soup without those two high-calorie ingredients.

2 teaspoons canola oil

1 onion, finely chopped

1 green bell pepper, seeded and finely chopped

1 celery stalk, finely chopped

1 garlic clove, minced

½ cup long-grain white rice

2 teaspoons Cajun seasoning

4 cups low-sodium chicken broth

1 (14½-ounce) can diced tomatoes

1 (10-ounce) box frozen sliced okra

1 cup thinly sliced cooked skinless chicken breast

MAKES 4 SERVINGS

1. Heat the oil in a large nonstick saucepan over medium-high heat. Add the onion, bell pepper, celery, and garlic. Cook, stirring occasionally, until the vegetables are softened, about 8 minutes. Stir in the rice and Cajun seasoning; cook 1 minute.

2. Add the broth, tomatoes, and okra; bring to a boil. Reduce the heat and simmer, partially covered, stirring occasionally, until the rice and okra are tender, about 15 minutes. Stir in the chicken and heat through.

PER SERVING (generous 2 cups): 272 Cal, 6 g Fat, 2 g Sat Fat, 0 g Trans Fat, 34 mg Chol, 320 mg Sod, 38 g Carb, 4 g Fib, 20 g Prot, 118 mg Calc. *POINTS* value: 5.

Take-Me-Out-to-the-Ball-Game Soup

Anne M. Rensberger, Washington, DC

"Losing weight on Weight Watchers is one of the most important achievements in my life!" proclaims Lifetime member, Anne. To help her stay on track, she needed to come to terms with her love for hot dogs smothered in sauerkraut that are often found at ball games. She did it by coming up with this incredibly tasty, low-*POINTS* value alternative. Serve with a slice of sourdough or rye bread on the side if you like, and up the *POINTS* value by 2.

1 teaspoon canola oil

1 onion, finely chopped

2 garlic cloves, minced

1 pound Italian turkey sausage, casings discarded, sausage crumbled

2 (8-ounce) cans sauerkraut, rinsed and drained

6 cups low-sodium chicken broth

MAKES 6 SERVINGS

1. Heat the oil in a large nonstick saucepan over medium-high heat. Add the onion and garlic and cook, stirring frequently, until translucent, 3–5 minutes. Add the sausage and cook, breaking up the sausage with a wooden spoon, until browned, about 8 minutes.

2. Add the sauerkraut and broth; bring to a boil. Reduce the heat and simmer, partially covered, until the sausage is cooked through, about 20 minutes.

PER SERVING (generous 1½ cups): 160 Cal, 7 g Fat, 2 g Sat Fat, 0 g Trans Fat, 49 mg Chol, 834 mg Sod, 8 g Carb, 2 g Fib, 16 g Prot, 43 mg Calc.
POINTS value: 3.

SOUPS AND SALADS

Italian Sausage Soup

Mary Beth Brinkerhoff, Avon, NY

Mary Beth likes to make this hearty and satisfying soup—a family favorite—ahead because it tastes even better the next day. It will keep in the refrigerator for up to two days or in the freezer for up to three months. "I love to cook and entertain," says Mary Beth, who also makes this "very popular" dish for lunch dates with friends.

1 tablespoon olive oil

½ pound fresh white mushrooms, thinly sliced

1 onion, chopped

1 carrot, chopped

2 garlic cloves, minced

1 pound sweet Italian turkey sausage, crumbled

4 cups low-sodium chicken broth

1 (14½-ounce) can no-salt added diced tomatoes

1 (8-ounce) can tomato sauce

1 zucchini, cubed

1 yellow squash, cubed

¼ pound fresh green beans, cut into 1½-inch pieces

½ (9-ounce) package fresh cheese tortellini

3 tablespoons minced basil

2 tablespoons grated Parmesan cheese

½ teaspoon ground pepper

MAKES 6 SERVINGS

1. Heat the oil in a large nonstick saucepan over medium-high heat. Add the mushrooms, onion, carrot, and garlic. Cook, stirring frequently, until the vegetables are tender, about 10 minutes. Add the sausage and cook, breaking up the sausage with a wooden spoon, until browned, about 8 minutes. Add the broth, tomatoes, and tomato sauce; bring to a boil. Reduce the heat and simmer, covered, until the flavors are blended, about 10 minutes.

2. Stir in the zucchini, yellow squash, green beans, and tortellini; return to a boil, stirring occasionally. Reduce the heat and simmer, covered, until the vegetables and tortellini are tender, about 8 minutes. Remove from the heat; stir in the basil, Parmesan cheese, and pepper.

PER SERVING (generous 1½ cups): 250 Cal, 9 g Fat, 3 g Sat Fat, 0 g Trans Fat, 53 mg Chol, 667 mg Sod, 24 g Carb, 5 g Fib, 21 g Prot, 109 mg Calc. *POINTS* value: 5.

tip You can use hot or smoked turkey sausage instead of the sweet sausage if you prefer.

ITALIAN SAUSAGE SOUP

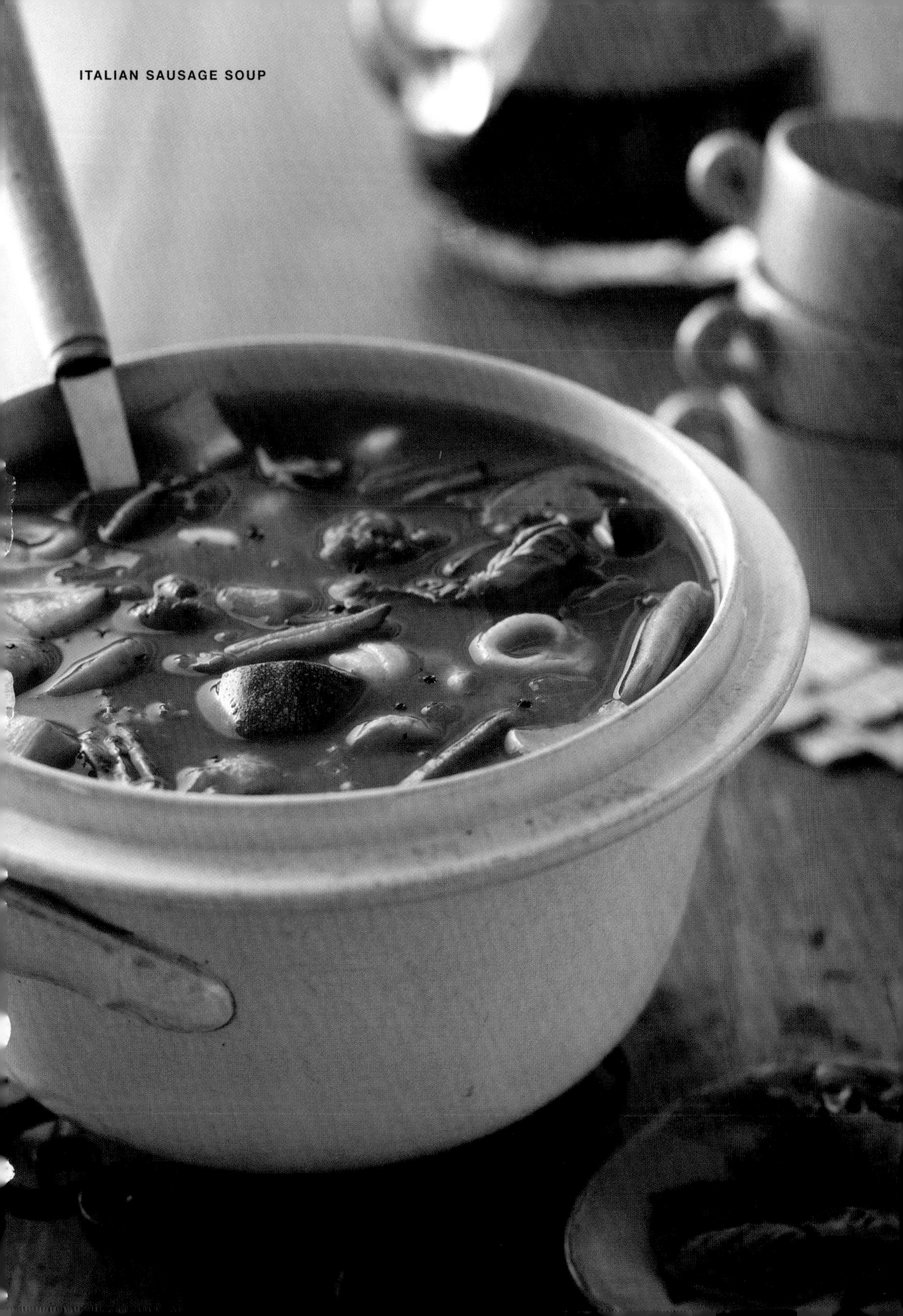

Spicy Lentil and Sausage Soup

Katherine Bolding, Henryetta, OK

Facing back surgery, Katherine was told that if she lost weight her recovery time would be shortened. She joined Weight Watchers and "with a supportive leader and encouragement from other members," she was able to lose close to 21 pounds. She had the surgery and recovered in minimum time! Here is just one of the delicious recipes that helped Katherine in her healthy pursuit.

1 tablespoon olive oil

1 onion, chopped

1 green bell pepper, seeded and chopped

4 ounces low-fat kielbasa, thinly sliced

2 garlic cloves, minced

1 teaspoon ground cumin

4 cups low-sodium chicken broth

1 cup dried brown lentils, picked over, rinsed, and drained

¾ cup prepared green or red salsa

1 all-purpose potato, peeled and cubed

1 yellow squash, cubed

2 tablespoons chopped fresh parsley

MAKES 6 SERVINGS

1. Heat the oil in a large nonstick saucepan over medium heat. Add the onion and bell pepper and cook, stirring frequently, until very tender, about 8 minutes. Add the kielbasa, garlic, and cumin; cook until fragrant, about 2 minutes. Add the broth, lentils, and salsa; bring to a boil. Reduce the heat and simmer, partially covered, until the lentils are almost tender, about 20 minutes.

2. Stir in the potato and squash; return to a boil. Reduce the heat and simmer, partially covered, until all of the vegetables and lentils are very tender, about 15 minutes. Remove from the heat and stir in the parsley.

PER SERVING (1⅓ cups): 227 Cal, 4 g Fat, 1 g Sat Fat, 0 g Trans Fat, 9 mg Chol, 333 mg Sod, 34 g Carb, 9 g Fib, 14 g Prot, 55 mg Calc. **POINTS** value: 4.

tip Green salsa or salsa verde, made with tomatillos, chiles, cilantro, and spices, is available fresh or in jars in most supermarkets.

Simply Elegant Salmon Chowder

Virginia C. Anthony, Jacksonville, FL

"I created this recipe when I had unexpected company for lunch and had all the ingredients on hand," says Virginia. Lucky company, we say. This rich-tasting, beautifully colored soup just might become a pantry-shelf standby for your unexpected guests or for a quick family supper. You could substitute chopped carrot or celery for the mushrooms, fat-free evaporated milk for the half-and-half, and parsley for the dill, if that's what's on hand in your kitchen.

1 onion, chopped

¼ pound fresh white mushrooms, thinly sliced

2 cups low-sodium chicken broth

1 medium red potato, unpeeled and cubed

1 (15¼-ounce) can whole kernel corn, drained

1½ cups fat-free half-and-half

1 (14¾-ounce) can salmon, drained and flaked

2 tablespoons chopped fresh dill

MAKES 6 SERVINGS

1. Spray a large nonstick saucepan with nonstick spray and set over medium heat. Add the onion and mushrooms and cook, stirring occasionally, until golden, about 8 minutes.

2. Add the broth and potato; bring to a boil. Reduce the heat and simmer, covered, until the potato is tender, about 12 minutes. Stir in the corn and half-and-half; return to a boil. Reduce the heat, stir in the salmon, and heat through. Remove from the heat and stir in the dill.

PER SERVING (generous 1 cup): 189 Cal, 6 g Fat, 1 g Sat Fat, 0 g Trans Fat, 37 mg Chol, 472 mg Sod, 20 g Carb, 2 g Fib, 16 g Prot, 170 mg Calc. *POINTS* value: **4.**

Easy Shrimp and Black Bean Soup

Kimberley M. West, Frankford, DE

"The inspiration for this recipe comes from my love of Mexican food," writes Kim, who is always looking for recipes to help on her "weight-loss journey." Full of fragrant and spicy southwestern flavors, this soup is especially easy to put together because Kim uses canned products and pre-cooked shrimp.

1 tablespoon olive oil

1 onion, chopped

2 garlic cloves, minced

2 teaspoons ground cumin

3 (15½-ounce) cans black beans, rinsed and drained

4 cups low-sodium chicken broth

1 (14½-ounce) can diced tomatoes

3 tablespoons canned chopped mild green chiles

1 (8-ounce) package frozen cooked salad shrimp, thawed

¼ cup chopped fresh cilantro

½ teaspoon hot pepper sauce

½ cup fat-free sour cream

Cilantro sprigs, for garnish

MAKES 6 SERVINGS

1. Heat the oil in a large nonstick saucepan over medium-high heat. Add the onion and cook, stirring frequently, until softened, about 6 minutes. Stir in the garlic and cumin. Cook until fragrant, about 1 minute.

2. Add the beans, broth, tomatoes, and chiles; bring to a boil. Reduce the heat and simmer, covered, until the flavors are blended and the soup thickens slightly, about 25 minutes. Puree one-third of the soup in a blender or food processor then stir the puree into the remaining soup. Add the shrimp, chopped cilantro, and hot pepper sauce; simmer until the shrimp is heated through, about 1 minute. Divide the soup among 6 bowls. Top evenly with the sour cream and top each with a cilantro sprig.

PER SERVING (1¾ cups soup with generous 1 tablespoon sour cream): 245 Cal, 5 g Fat, 1 g Sat Fat, 0 g Trans Fat, 78 mg Chol, 549 mg Sod, 29 g Carb, 9 g Fib, 20 g Prot, 118 mg Calc. *POINTS* value: *5.*

French Onion Soup

Michelle Norwood, Auburndale, FL

French onion soup gets its distinctive flavor from the long, slow cooking of the onions—their natural sugars caramelize and the flavor becomes mildly sweet. Use naturally sweet Vidalia onions or substitute yellow onions and add a teaspoon of sugar to help bring out the sweetness. "If you want to lower the **POINTS** value by 3, leave out the bread and cheese. The soup still tastes great without it," says Michelle.

1 tablespoon olive oil

6 Vidalia onions, thinly sliced

1 tablespoon Worcestershire
  sauce

6 cups low-sodium beef broth

½ cup dry red wine

¼ teaspoon dried thyme

6 (2-inch) slices Italian bread,
  toasted

3 (1-ounce) slices reduced-fat
  Swiss cheese, each cut
  in half

MAKES 6 SERVINGS

1. Heat the oil in a large nonstick saucepan over medium-high heat. Add the onions and cook, stirring occasionally, until softened, about 10 minutes. Stir in the Worcestershire sauce. Reduce the heat to low and cook, stirring occasionally, until the onions are very soft and golden, about 25 minutes.

2. Add the broth, wine, and thyme; bring to a boil. Reduce the heat and simmer, partially covered, until the flavors are blended, about 40 minutes.

3. Preheat the oven to 450°F. Place 6 (10-ounce) ovenproof bowls on a jelly-roll pan. Place a slice of the toast in each soup bowl. Pour the soup gently over the bread and top each with a half slice of the cheese. Bake until the cheese is golden and the soup is bubbly, 10–15 minutes.

PER SERVING (generous 1 cup with bread and cheese): 308 Cal, 9 g Fat, 3 g Sat Fat, 0 g Trans Fat, 9 mg Chol, 309 mg Sod, 44 g Carb, 7 g Fib, 15 g Prot, 249 mg Calc. **POINTS** value: **6.**

SOUPS AND SALADS

Cauliflower Cheese Soup

Colleen Armstrong, Cayuga, Ontario, Canada

Colleen has lost 27 pounds on the At Work Program®. "It's great to have so much support all day from the people you work with," she says. She enriches her soup with a little light cream cheese and American cheese, making it a creamy, delicately flavored appetizer soup or a light lunch. Try serving with short breadsticks (2 will increase the *POINTS* value by 1).

2 teaspoons olive oil

1 leek (about 6 ounces), cleaned and sliced (white and light green parts only)

1 carrot, finely chopped

1 celery stalk, finely chopped

5 cups low-sodium chicken broth

4 cups cauliflower florets

1 (¾-ounce) slice reduced-fat American pasteurized cheese food

2 tablespoons light (Neufchâtel) cream cheese, at room temperature

2 tablespoons chopped fresh chives

MAKES 6 SERVINGS

1. Heat the oil in a large nonstick saucepan over medium heat. Add the leek, carrot, and celery. Cook, stirring frequently, until the vegetables are very tender, but not browned, about 8 minutes.

2. Add the broth and cauliflower; bring to a boil. Reduce the heat and simmer, covered, until the cauliflower is very tender, about 30 minutes. Stir in the cheeses until melted.

3. Remove the soup from the heat and puree with a hand-held immersion blender, or in a food processor or blender, in batches if necessary. Return the soup to the saucepan and reheat. Stir in the chives.

PER SERVING (1⅓ cups): 91 Cal, 5 g Fat, 2 g Sat Fat, 0 g Trans Fat, 9 mg Chol, 190 mg Sod, 8 g Carb, 3 g Fib, 6 g Prot, 68 mg Calc. *POINTS* value: *2*.

tip A hand-held immersion blender comes in handy in this recipe since it allows you to puree the soup right in the pan, rather than having to transfer it to a food processor or blender.

SOUPS AND SALADS

Italian Spinach and Egg Drop Soup

Janel L. Tortorice, North Brunswick, NJ

"This is an old family recipe. I make it after a long hard day when I don't want to fuss, but still want something that's good and satisfying. It's the perfect comfort food for me," writes Janel, who has lost over 40 pounds on the Weight Watchers program. You could make it even more fuss-free by using half a package of frozen chopped spinach, thawed, instead of the fresh spinach.

4 cups low-sodium
   chicken broth
½ cup small shell macaroni
1 large egg, lightly beaten
2 tablespoons grated
   Parmesan cheese
Pinch nutmeg
4 cups baby spinach leaves,
   coarsely chopped

MAKES 2 SERVINGS

1. Bring the broth to a boil over medium-high heat in a large saucepan. Add the macaroni; return to a boil. Reduce the heat and simmer, uncovered, until the macaroni is tender, 8–10 minutes.

2. Combine the egg, cheese, and nutmeg in a small bowl. Slowly pour the egg mixture into the simmering soup, stirring constantly with a fork until the egg forms shreds. Stir in the spinach and heat through.

PER SERVING (2 cups): 216 Cal, 8 g Fat, 4 g Sat Fat, 0 g Trans Fat, 118 mg Chol, 388 mg Sod, 22 g Carb, 2 g Fib, 16 g Prot, 176 mg Calc. *POINTS* value: **5.**

Bean Burrito Soup

Leslee Hildebrand, Columbus, OH

The whole family will love this "burrito in a bowl"—a yummy soup of chunky vegetables, beans, and broth, colorfully topped with strips of tortilla, shredded cheese, sour cream, and cilantro. Leslee uses canned beans and frozen mixed vegetables, which makes this easy and ready to eat in just minutes.

2 cups low-sodium chicken broth

1 (16-ounce) can fat-free refried beans

1 (16-ounce) bag frozen mixed vegetables

2 tablespoons canned chopped mild green chiles

2 garlic cloves, minced

1 tablespoon chili powder

1 (6-inch) fat-free flour tortilla, cut into thin strips (about ½ cup)

6 tablespoons shredded reduced-fat cheddar cheese

6 tablespoons fat-free sour cream

3 tablespoons chopped fresh cilantro

MAKES 4 SERVINGS

1. Bring the broth and beans to a boil in a large saucepan over medium-high heat. Add the mixed vegetables, chiles, garlic, and chili powder; return to a boil. Reduce the heat and simmer, covered, until the flavors are blended and the vegetables are tender, about 6 minutes.

2. Divide the soup evenly among 4 bowls. Top each bowl with about 2 tablespoons tortilla strips, 1½ tablespoons each of cheese and sour cream, then a sprinkling of chopped cilantro.

PER SERVING (1½ cups soup with toppings): 250 Cal, 4 g Fat, 2 g Sat Fat, 0 g Trans Fat, 12 mg Chol, 639 mg Sod, 40 g Carb, 12 g Fib, 15 g Prot, 200 mg Calc. *POINTS* value: 5.

Pasta e Fagioli

Melanie Lehman, Peoria, AZ

After tasting this hearty pasta-and-bean soup at a favorite Italian restaurant, Melanie, who has lost 49 pounds on the program, was inspired to make a Weight Watchers version at home. "After several tries, I finally came up with this delicious solution," says Melanie. "My neighbors and Weight Watchers friends love it!"

1 tablespoon canola oil

1 onion, chopped

1 carrot, chopped

1 celery stalk, chopped

2 garlic cloves, minced

½ pound lean ground beef (10% or less fat)

1 teaspoon chili powder

1 (14½-ounce) can diced tomatoes

4 cups low-sodium chicken broth

½ cup small shell pasta

1 (15½-ounce) can Great Northern beans, rinsed and drained

3 tablespoons grated Parmesan cheese

½ teaspoon freshly ground pepper

MAKES 6 SERVINGS

1. Heat the oil in a large nonstick saucepan over medium heat. Add the onion, carrot, celery, and garlic. Cook, stirring frequently, until the vegetables are soft, about 10 minutes. Add the ground beef and cook, stirring occasionally, until browned, about 5 minutes. Stir in the chili powder; cook 1 minute. Add the tomatoes and bring to a boil. Reduce the heat and simmer, uncovered, stirring occasionally, until the tomatoes are softened and the liquid has evaporated, about 10 minutes.

2. Stir in the broth and pasta; bring to a boil. Reduce the heat and simmer, partially covered, until the pasta is tender and the soup thickens slightly, about 8 minutes. Add the beans and heat though. Remove from the heat, then sprinkle with the cheese and pepper.

PER SERVING (generous 1 cup): 191 Cal, 6 g Fat, 2 g Sat Fat, 1 g Trans Fat, 12 mg Chol, 675 mg Sod, 21 g Carb, 5 g Fib, 14 g Prot, 79 mg Calc. *POINTS* value: 4.

Hint O' Hot Split Pea Soup

Julie Brandt, Indian Rocks Beach, FL

Julie is a vegetarian and serves this hearty and spicy soup (it gets its hint of heat from a generous dose of cayenne) for dinner with salad and fresh bread. "This is my very first recipe that I've created from scratch," says Julie. "My husband used to tease me, saying he cooked better than I did. He's eating his words—and my soup—now."

1 tablespoon vegetable oil

1 onion, chopped

1 carrot, chopped

1 celery stalk, chopped

2 garlic cloves, minced

8 cups low-sodium vegetable broth

2 medium all-purpose potatoes, peeled and cubed

2 cups dried split peas, picked over, rinsed, and drained

½ teaspoon salt

½ teaspoon dried thyme

½ teaspoon cayenne

1 bay leaf

MAKES 6 SERVINGS

1. Heat the oil in a large nonstick saucepan over medium-high heat. Add the onion, carrot, celery, and garlic. Cook, stirring frequently, until softened, about 6 minutes.

2. Add the broth, potatoes, split peas, salt, thyme, cayenne, and bay leaf; bring to a boil. Reduce the heat and simmer, covered, until all the vegetables are very tender and the split peas are soft, 45–50 minutes. Discard the bay leaf before serving.

PER SERVING (1¾ cups): 312 Cal, 5 g Fat, 1 g Sat Fat, 0 g Trans Fat, 0 mg Chol, 358 mg Sod, 50 g Carb, 16 g Fib, 18 g Prot, 61 mg Calc. *POINTS* value: **6.**

Corn Chowder

Sandra Banas, Brunswick, ME

Sandra finds the **POINTS** value program makes the job of losing weight easier. She has lost 11 pounds—with the help of this favorite soup of hers. Originally a chunky seafood soup, the term chowder is also used to describe any thick soup, usually containing chunks of potatoes and a variety of other vegetables. When in season, nothing beats corn chowder, made with crisp, sweet, fresh corn. So if you've got them, substitute the kernels shucked from six ears of fresh corn for the canned in this recipe. One ear of corn will give you about $\frac{1}{2}$ cup of kernels.

3 slices bacon, coarsely chopped

2 teaspoons olive oil

1 onion, chopped

1 red bell pepper, seeded and diced

1 pound all-purpose potatoes, peeled and diced

4 cups low-sodium chicken broth

¼ teaspoon salt

¼ teaspoon paprika

1 (15¼-ounce) can whole-kernel corn, drained

1 (14¾-ounce) can creamed-style corn

1 cup fat-free evaporated milk

3–4 drops hot pepper sauce

2 tablespoons chopped scallions

MAKES 6 SERVINGS

1. Heat a small nonstick skillet over medium-high heat. Add the bacon and cook until crisp, about 4 minutes. Transfer the bacon to paper towels to drain; set aside.

2. Heat the oil in a large nonstick saucepan over medium-high heat. Add the onion and bell pepper and cook, stirring frequently, until softened, about 6 minutes. Add the potatoes, broth, salt, and paprika; bring to a boil. Reduce the heat and simmer, covered, until the potatoes are soft, about 20 minutes.

3. Add the corn, creamed corn, evaporated milk, and hot pepper sauce; return to a boil. Reduce the heat and simmer, covered, about 2 minutes. Remove from the heat and stir in the scallions.

PER SERVING (generous 1⅓ cups): 246 Cal, 5 g Fat, 1 g Sat Fat, 0 g Trans Fat, 7 mg Chol, 627 mg Sod, 43 g Carb, 4 g Fib, 10 g Prot, 149 mg Calc. POINTS value: 5.

SOUPS AND SALADS

Sweet Potato and Leek Soup

Heather Kamins, Oakland, CA

Leek soup is traditionally made with white potatoes, but here's a delicious twist on the old favorite. The result—a velvety, slightly sweet, and colorful soup that makes a great first course for a fall dinner or Thanksgiving feast.

1 tablespoon olive oil

2 leeks (about ¾ pound), cleaned and sliced (white and light green parts only)

1 garlic clove, minced

3 sweet potatoes (about 1½ pounds), peeled and cubed

6 cups low-sodium chicken broth

¼ cup fat-free half-and-half

Pinch nutmeg

¼ cup chopped fresh chives

MAKES 6 SERVINGS

1. Heat the oil in a large nonstick saucepan over medium heat. Add the leeks and garlic and cook, stirring frequently, until the leeks are tender, about 6 minutes. Add the sweet potatoes and broth; bring to a boil. Reduce the heat and simmer, covered, stirring occasionally, until the potatoes are fork-tender, about 25 minutes.

2. Remove the pan from the heat; let the mixture cool for a few minutes. Transfer the mixture in batches to a blender or food processor and puree. Return the soup to the pan. Stir in the half-and-half and nutmeg; return to a simmer. Serve sprinkled with the chives.

PER SERVING (1⅓ cups): 167 Cal, 4 g Fat, 1 g Sat Fat, 0 g Trans Fat, 4 mg Chol, 133 mg Sod, 28 g Carb, 2 g Fib, 5 g Prot, 65 mg Calc. **POINTS** value: **3.**

tip Leeks often contain sand in between their layers. Here's how to clean them: Trim away most of the dark green tops and the roots, leaving the root end intact to hold the layers together. Slice the leek lengthwise to within a half inch of the root end. Hold the leek by the root end, fan open the layers, and rinse thoroughly under cold running water.

Carrot-Orange Soup

Susanne Dutcher, Deerfield, IL

Susie lost 29 pounds on the At Work Program by taking a recipe such as this—originally from a French restaurant, "containing a whole stick of butter"—and revising it according to Weight Watchers guidelines. She and her family like this soup so much, she is including it in her own cookbook created for her "treasured daughter-in-law" who, "just like this soup, is colorful, warm, and refreshing."

1 tablespoon vegetable oil

2 pounds carrots, chopped

1 large onion, chopped

1 teaspoon ground cumin

6 cups low-sodium vegetable or chicken broth

2 teaspoons grated orange zest

½ cup fresh orange juice

¼ teaspoon nutmeg

2 scallions, thinly sliced diagonally

MAKES 6 SERVINGS

1. Heat the oil in a large nonstick saucepan over medium heat. Add the carrots and onion and cook, partially covered, stirring occasionally, until the carrots and onion are softened, about 10 minutes. Stir in the cumin and cook about 1 minute.

2. Stir in the broth; bring to a boil. Reduce the heat and simmer, uncovered, until the carrots are very tender, about 25 minutes.

3. Remove the pan from the heat; let the mixture cool for a few minutes. Transfer the mixture in batches to a food processor or blender and puree. Return the soup to the pan. Stir in the orange zest, juice, and nutmeg; return to a simmer. Remove from the heat; stir in the scallions.

PER SERVING (1⅓ cups): 143 Cal, 4 g Fat, 1 g Sat Fat, 0 g Trans Fat, 0 mg Chol, 188 mg Sod, 22 g Carb, 5 g Fib, 6 g Prot, 69 mg Calc. *POINTS* value: 2.

SOUPS AND SALADS

Butternut Squash Soup

Theresa Thompson, Fort Worth, TX

A recent Lifetime member, Theresa credits Weight Watchers with "helping me to learn about proper portion sizes and healthy food choices." She says the meetings and support from other members are the keys to her success. This delicious soup, filled with the robust fall flavors of squash, leek, parsnip, and apple, is a good example of the healthy food choices she makes. Substitute pumpkin for the butternut squash if you like.

6 cups low-sodium
   chicken broth
1 large butternut squash (about
   3 pounds), peeled, seeded,
   and cut into
   1-inch cubes
1 medium leek, cleaned and
   sliced (white and light green
   parts only)
1 parsnip, peeled and cut into
   ½-inch slices
1 Granny Smith apple, peeled,
   cored, and chopped
¼ cup fat-free half-and-half
1½ teaspoons curry powder
½ teaspoon salt
2 tablespoons chopped
   fresh chives

MAKES 4 SERVINGS

1. Bring the broth to a boil over medium-high heat in a large saucepan. Add the squash, leek, parsnip, and apple; return to a boil. Reduce the heat and simmer, partially covered, until the squash is soft enough to mash easily, about 25 minutes.

2. Remove the pan from the heat; let the mixture cool for a few minutes. Transfer the mixture in batches to a food processor or blender and puree. Return the soup to the pan. Stir in the half-and-half, curry powder, and salt; return to a simmer. Remove from the heat and stir in the chives.

PER SERVING (1⅓ cups): 120 Cal, 2 g Fat, 1 g Sat Fat, 0 g Trans Fat, 3 mg Chol, 243 mg Sod, 25 g Carb, 6 g Fib, 4 g Prot, 98 mg Calc. **POINTS** value: 2.

tip To peel the squash, cut in half crosswise, separating the narrow top part of the squash from the round bottom part. This step makes it easier to handle the squash. Remove the seeds then, using a very sharp, sturdy vegetable peeler or a sharp knife, cut the skin away from the squash.

Zesty Broccoli Soup

Linda Danielson, North Mankato, MN

"Weight Watchers has taught me a lot about portion control and writing down what I eat," writes Linda. She often serves this low-*POINTS* value soup before dinner. It's wonderful hot or cold. To save on prep time, you can use two (10-ounce) packages of frozen chopped broccoli or broccoli spears instead of the fresh broccoli.

6 cups low-sodium chicken or
vegetable broth

1¼ pounds broccoli crowns, cut
into florets (6 cups)

3 all-purpose potatoes (about
1 pound), peeled and cubed

1 onion, chopped

1 celery stalk, chopped

½ teaspoon salt

1 cup fat-free milk

2 drops hot pepper sauce

MAKES 6 SERVINGS

1. Bring the broth to a boil over medium-high heat in a large saucepan. Add the broccoli, potatoes, onion, celery, and salt; return to a boil. Reduce the heat and simmer, partially covered, until the vegetables are soft enough to mash, about 25 minutes.

2. Remove the pan from the heat and let the mixture cool slightly. Transfer the mixture in batches to a food processor or blender and puree. Return the soup to the pan. Stir in the milk, and hot pepper sauce, then return to a simmer.

PER SERVING (generous 1½ cups): 133 Cal, 2 g Fat, 1 g Sat Fat, 0 g Trans Fat, 5 mg Chol, 355 mg Sod, 23 g Carb, 4 g Fib, 8 g Prot, 112 mg Calc. *POINTS* value: 2.

Florentine Tomato Soup

Arlene Wizwer, Chelmsford, MA

Arlene took inspiration from her "wonderful Weight Watchers leader" to create this delicious soup, which Arlene loves to serve on a chilly winter night. If you prefer, use escarole, savoy cabbage, or any green leafy vegetable instead of the spinach— and any short, tubular pasta, such as ditalini or tubetti or even orzo, could replace the macaroni.

1 tablespoon olive oil

1 onion, chopped

2 garlic cloves, minced

1 (14½-ounce) can diced tomatoes

4 cups low-sodium vegetable or chicken broth

¾ cup small shell macaroni

½ teaspoon salt

2 cups baby spinach leaves, coarsely chopped

½ teaspoon freshly ground pepper

2 tablespoons grated Parmesan cheese

MAKES 4 SERVINGS

1. Heat the oil in a large nonstick saucepan over medium heat. Add the onion and garlic and cook, stirring frequently, until the onion is very tender, about 8 minutes. Stir in the tomatoes; bring to a boil. Reduce the heat and simmer, uncovered, stirring occasionally, until the tomatoes are softened and the liquid is reduced by about half, about 5 minutes.

2. Stir in the broth, macaroni, and salt; bring to a boil. Reduce the heat and simmer, uncovered, until the macaroni is tender, 8–10 minutes. Stir in the spinach and pepper. Cook until the spinach just begins to wilt, about 30 seconds. Remove from the heat. Serve sprinkled with the cheese.

PER SERVING (1½ cups soup and ½ tablespoon cheese): 174 Cal, 6 g Fat, 2 g Sat Fat, 0 g Trans Fat, 6 mg Chol, 590 mg Sod, 24 g Carb, 3 g Fib, 8 g Prot, 96 mg Calc. *POINTS* value: **3**.

SOUPS AND SALADS

Spicy Roasted Red Pepper Soup

Anne Loving Waynesboro, PA

Anne teaches third grade and has a deal with a fellow teacher to bring a Weight Watchers-style lunch for the two of them almost everyday. In return, her fellow teacher pays Anne what she would pay for a school lunch. "This soup is her favorite," says Anne.

4 red bell peppers

1 tablespoon olive oil

1 onion, chopped

2 garlic cloves, minced

5 cups low-sodium vegetable or chicken broth

1 teaspoon chili-garlic sauce

½ teaspoon salt

¼ cup fat-free half-and-half

3 tablespoons chopped fresh basil

MAKES 4 SERVINGS

1. Preheat the broiler. Line the broiler pan with foil; place the peppers on the pan. Broil 5 inches from the heat, turning frequently with tongs, until the skins are lightly charred, 10–20 minutes. Place the peppers in a large bowl; cover with plastic wrap and let steam 10 minutes. When cool enough to handle, peel. Then cut each pepper in half and discard seeds. Coarsely chop the peppers; set aside.

2. Heat the oil in a large nonstick saucepan over medium-high heat. Add the onion and garlic. Cook, stirring frequently, until the onion is tender, about 8 minutes. Stir in the roasted peppers, the broth, garlic sauce, and salt; bring to a boil. Reduce the heat and simmer, partially covered, until the peppers are very soft and the flavors are blended, about 10 minutes.

3. Remove the pan from the heat; let the mixture cool for a few minutes. Transfer the mixture in batches to a food processor or blender and puree. Return the soup to the pan. Stir in the half-and-half and return to a simmer. Remove from the heat and stir in the basil.

PER SERVING (1¾ cups): 129 Cal, 6 g Fat, 2 g Sat Fat, 0 g Trans Fat, 4 mg Chol, 495 mg Sod, 15 g Carb, 3 g Fib, 6 g Prot, 64 mg Calc. *POINTS* value: 2.

SOUPS AND SALADS

EDAMAME SALAD

Edamame Salad

Carolyn S. Greenfield, Arlington, VA

After reading about the great nutritional properties of edamame (green soybeans), Carolyn, who has lost 36 pounds, was inspired to substitute them for the beans in a favorite bean salad recipe of hers. She is very happy with the result, saying, "It's very healthy and low in calories while at the same time tasty and filling. What more can you wish for if you're trying to shed pounds?" She frequently adds chopped red bell pepper to the salad for color, flavor, and additional nutrients. Garnish with thin slivers of lemon peel, if you like.

1 (12-ounce) bag fresh or frozen shelled edamame

1 tablespoon fresh lemon juice

1 teaspoon Dijon mustard

1 tablespoon extra-virgin olive oil

1 garlic clove, minced

¼ teaspoon salt

¼ teaspoon freshly ground pepper

MAKES 4 SERVINGS

1. Bring a large pot of water to a boil. Add the edamame, return to a boil, and cook until just crisp-tender, 6–8 minutes. Rinse under cold running water, drain, and place in a large bowl.

2. To make the dressing, combine the lemon juice, mustard, oil, garlic, salt, and pepper in a small bowl. Pour the dressing over the beans. Serve at once, or cover and refrigerate until ready to serve, up to 2 days.

PER SERVING (¾ cup): 147 Cal, 6 g Fat, 1 g Sat Fat, 0 g Trans Fat, 0 mg Chol, 212 mg Sod, 12 g Carb, 4 g Fib, 9 g Prot, 60 mg Calc. **POINTS** value: **3.**

tip Edamame can be purchased fresh from Asian markets and some produce markets but are most often found in the frozen-food section of supermarkets. Fresh edamame should be used within two days. Frozen will last for several months.

Southwestern Layered Salad

Glenna Williams, Longview, TX

Glenna feels that "part of the enjoyment of food is in the appearance," which is why she likes to serve this pretty salad. You'll want to show off the colorful layers by serving it in a clear glass bowl. It's perfect for a potluck supper, company picnic, or luncheon buffet.

1 (15½-ounce) can black beans, rinsed and drained

¼ cup prepared salsa

¼ cup chopped fresh cilantro

2 cups finely chopped romaine lettuce

2 medium tomatoes, chopped

1 (15¼-ounce) can whole-kernel corn, drained

1 green bell pepper, seeded and diced

1 red onion, finely chopped

½ cup shredded reduced-fat cheddar cheese

½ avocado, peeled and cut into ¼-inch slices

2 slices reduced-sodium bacon, cooked and crumbled

¼ cup fat-free Italian dressing

MAKES 8 SERVINGS

1. Combine the beans, salsa, and 2 tablespoons of the cilantro in a small bowl. Layer the ingredients in a 1½-quart clear glass bowl in this order: the bean mixture, lettuce, tomatoes, corn, bell pepper, onion, and cheese.

2. Just before serving, arrange the avocado on top. Sprinkle with the bacon and the remaining 2 tablespoons cilantro. Drizzle the salad with the dressing.

PER SERVING (1⅓ cups): 166 Cal, 6 g Fat, 2 g Sat Fat, 0 g Trans Fat, 9 mg Chol, 396 mg Sod, 23 g Carb, 6 g Fib, 8 g Prot, 106 mg Calc. *POINTS* value: **3**.

tip Here's an easy way to slice avocados without peeling. After cutting the avocado in half and removing the pit, slice through the flesh, but not the skin with a paring knife. Run a rubber spatula around the circumference, just inside the skin, to loosen the flesh, then gently twist the spatula to pop out the flesh.

SOUTHWESTERN LAYERED SALAD

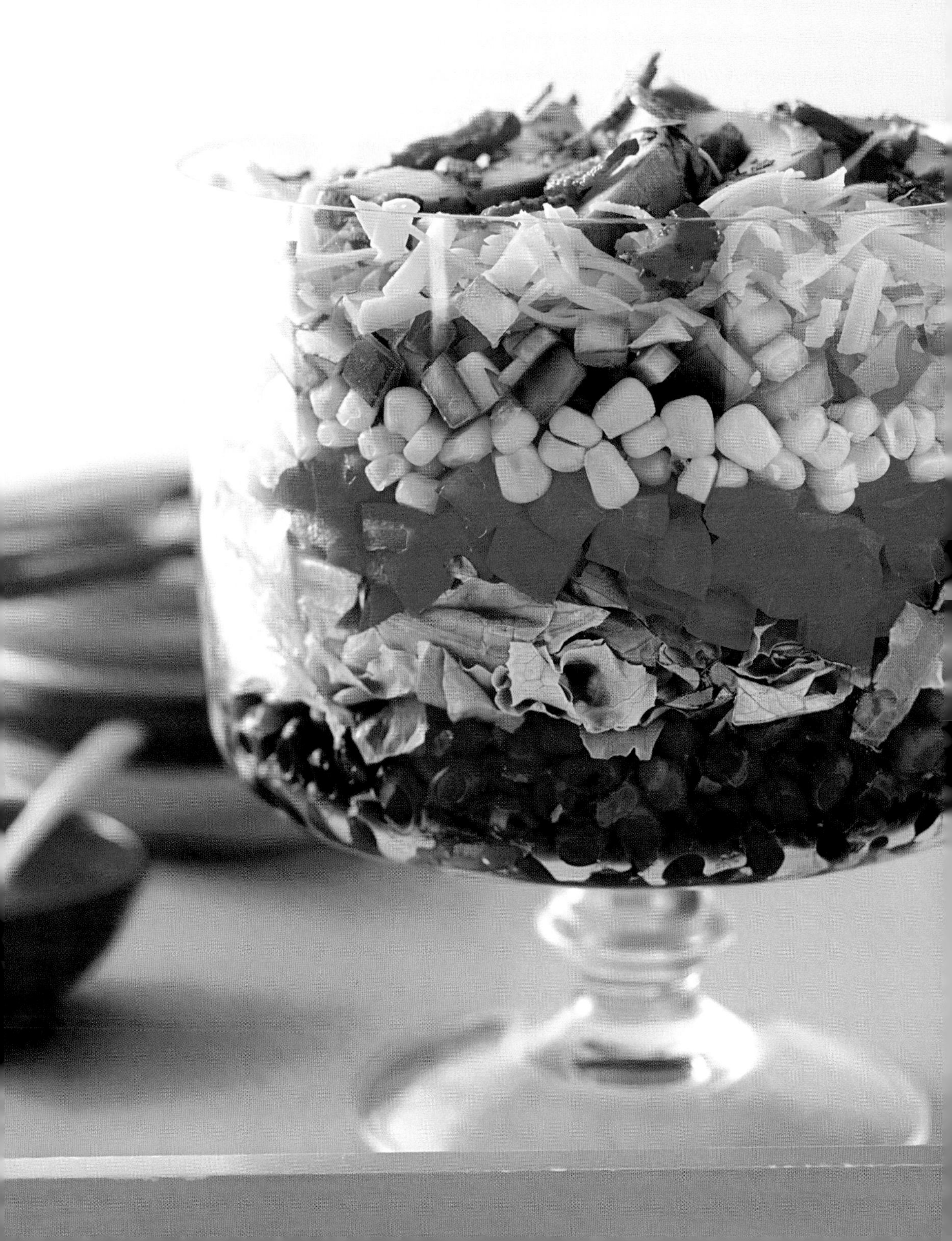

Black-Eyed Pea Salad

Judy Glass, Boynton Beach, FL

Judy, who loves salads, has lost over 27 pounds so far on Weight Watchers. This simple, inexpensive salad is often euphemistically referred to as "Texas caviar" in the southern United States. Though you can serve it right away, Judy suggests making it a day ahead, if you can, to allow its flavors to blend fully. If you can't find black-eyed peas, canned white beans, pinto beans, or even cooked lentils work just as well.

2 tablespoons cider vinegar

2 teaspoons olive oil

1 garlic clove, minced

½ teaspoon sugar

½ teaspoon freshly
   ground pepper

¼ teaspoon salt

4 drops hot pepper sauce

1 (15½-ounce) can black-eyed
   peas, rinsed and drained

1 red onion, diced

1 green bell pepper, seeded
   and diced

1 red bell pepper, seeded
   and diced

2 celery stalks, diced

Red or green leaf lettuce leaves

MAKES 4 SERVINGS

1. Whisk the vinegar, oil, garlic, sugar, pepper, salt, and hot pepper sauce in a large bowl. Add the black-eyed peas, onion, bell peppers, and celery. Serve at once or cover and refrigerate for up to 3 days.

2. To serve, line a serving plate with the lettuce leaves and top with the salad.

PER SERVING (1 cup): 118 Cal, 3 g Fat, 0 g Sat Fat, 0 g Trans Fat, 0 mg Chol, 290 mg Sod, 20 g Carb, 5 g Fib, 5 g Prot, 45 mg Calc. *POINTS* value: 2.

Brown Rice Salad

Robbie Osterberg, Cambria, CA

The Weight Watchers program is "a plan I can live with," says Robbie, who is a Lifetime member with a weight loss of 34 pounds. Robbie's daughter urged him to submit this delicious, healthful, and colorful rice salad, which he likes to serve, mostly in the summer, on a bed of lettuce with sliced tomatoes for lunch. It also makes a good side dish to serve with grilled fish or chicken.

2¼ cups low-sodium chicken broth

1 cup brown rice

3 tablespoons reduced-sodium soy sauce

1 tablespoon seasoned rice vinegar

1 tablespoon fresh lemon juice

1 tablespoon olive oil

1 cup frozen peas, thawed

1 red bell pepper, seeded and diced

1 carrot, diced

1 celery stalk, diced

4 scallions, thinly sliced

¼ cup golden raisins

2 tablespoons chopped fresh parsley

MAKES 6 SERVINGS

1. Bring the broth to a boil in a medium saucepan. Stir in the rice. Reduce the heat and simmer, covered, until all the liquid is absorbed and the rice is tender, about 45 minutes. Remove from the heat; let stand, covered, about 10 minutes.

2. Whisk the soy sauce, vinegar, lemon juice, and oil in a large bowl. Add the rice, peas, bell pepper, carrot, celery, scallions, raisins, and parsley; toss well to coat. Serve at once while still warm or cover and refrigerate until ready to serve, up to 2 days.

PER SERVING (1 cup): 212 Cal, 4 g Fat, 1 g Sat Fat, 0 g Trans Fat, 1 mg Chol, 440 mg Sod, 38 g Carb, 5 g Fib, 7 g Prot, 42 mg Calc. **POINTS** value: **4**.

tip If you would like to save time, use quick-cooking brown rice.

SOUPS AND SALADS

Wild Rice Salad with Orzo and Cranberries

Stacey Lorenson, Mission Viejo, CA

Stacey likes her recipe because "It's very healthy and satisfies the Weight Watchers goal of adding more whole grains, fruits, and veggies to the diet." The tart apple, sweet oranges, and dried cranberries contrast well with the nutty flavor of wild rice. Raspberry vinegar complements this salad nicely, but red-wine vinegar works well too.

2 cups water
½ cup wild rice
½ cup orzo
2 navel oranges, peeled and cut into sections
1 Granny Smith apple, chopped
1 celery stalk, finely chopped
¼ cup dried cranberries
2 tablespoons chopped fresh parsley
2 tablespoons raspberry vinegar
1 tablespoon olive oil
½ teaspoon salt
¼ teaspoon freshly ground pepper

MAKES 4 SERVINGS

1. Bring the water to a boil in a medium saucepan. Stir in the rice. Reduce the heat and simmer, covered, until tender, about 45 minutes. Drain and transfer to a large bowl.

2. Bring a medium pot of lightly salted water to a boil. Add the orzo and cook until tender, about 10 minutes; drain. Rinse under running cold water; drain well and add to the bowl with the wild rice. Add the oranges, apple, celery, cranberries, parsley, vinegar, oil, salt, and pepper; toss well to coat. Serve at once or cover and refrigerate until ready to serve, up to 2 days.

PER SERVING (1¼ cups): 266 Cal, 4 g Fat, 1 g Sat Fat, 0 g Trans Fat, 0 mg Chol, 309 mg Sod, 52 g Carb, 6 g Fib, 7 g Prot, 45 mg Calc. **POINTS** value: *5.*

tip To section an orange, use a sharp paring knife and slice away the top and bottom ends of the orange. Put the orange on a cutting board and slice away the rind, removing all of the white pith. Working over a small bowl to catch the juices, cut the orange sections out from between the membranes, letting each piece fall into the bowl as you cut it free. Discard seeds.

Summer Corn Salad

Susan Murtaugh, Two Rivers, WI

Susan says, "I love my meetings. I look forward to seeing everyone week after week." The meetings obviously work for her—she has lost "73 pounds and counting." Susan likes to serve this refreshing and colorful salad (for which she gets "rave reviews") with toasted pita wedges, in a tortilla with lettuce and hummus, or as an accompaniment to grilled shrimp.

4 fresh corn, husks and silks removed, or 1 (10-ounce package) frozen whole-kernel corn, thawed

1 large tomato, seeded and diced

½ cucumber, peeled, seeded, and diced

1 green bell pepper, seeded and diced

4 scallions, thinly sliced

4 radishes, thinly sliced

3 tablespoons chopped fresh cilantro

3 tablespoons seasoned rice vinegar

½ teaspoon salt

¼ teaspoon freshly ground pepper

MAKES 4 SERVINGS

Cut the kernels from the corn cobs and place in a large bowl. Add the tomato, cucumber, bell pepper, scallions, radishes, cilantro, vinegar, salt, and pepper; gently toss to coat. Cover and refrigerate at least 1 hour before serving.

PER SERVING (generous 1 cup): 114 Cal, 1 g Fat, 0 g Sat Fat, 0 g Trans Fat, 0 mg Chol, 538 mg Sod, 26 g Carb, 4 g Fib, 4 g Prot, 23 mg Calc. *POINTS* value: *2.*

tip To remove the kernels from fresh corn, cut the husked ear crosswise in half so that the ear has a flat surface to stand on while you work. Then, using a sharp knife, cut down along the outside. One ear of corn will yield about ¹/₂ cup kernels.

SOUPS AND SALADS

My Big Fat Greek Salad

Rose Roach, Melbourne, FL

"I have been concocting salads for many years and I just kept adding ingredients to this one until I found a flavorful combination," writes Rose. Her friends love this veggie-packed, flavorful salad and always request that she brings it to potlucks.

½ pound eggplant,

3 tablespoons balsamic vinegar

1 tablespoon olive oil

1 garlic clove, minced

1 teaspoon Dijon mustard

¾ teaspoon dried oregano

½ teaspoon salt

1 (10-ounce) bag romaine lettuce, torn

1 tomato, seeded and chopped

1 small cucumber, peeled, seeded, and diced

½ (14-ounce) can artichoke hearts, drained and quartered

½ red onion, thinly sliced

2 tablespoons mild pepper rings, drained

2 tablespoons chopped pimientos

10 kalamata olives, chopped

3 tablespoons reduced-fat feta cheese

MAKES 6 SERVINGS

1. Spray the broiler rack with nonstick spray; preheat the broiler. Cut the eggplant into ¼-inch-thick slices; place on the broiler rack and lightly spray with nonstick spray. Broil, 5 inches from the heat, until golden and tender, about 4 minutes on each side.

2. Whisk the vinegar, oil, garlic, mustard, oregano, and salt, in a large bowl. Add the lettuce, tomato, cucumber, artichoke hearts, onion, pepper rings, and pimientos; toss gently to coat. Top the salad with the eggplant slices, then sprinkle with the olives and feta cheese, and serve at once.

PER SERVING (1¾ cups): 90 Cal, 5 g Fat, 1 g Sat Fat, 0 g Trans Fat, 1 mg Chol, 432 mg Sod, 10 g Carb, 3 g Fib, 3 g Prot, 43 mg Calc. **POINTS** value: 2.

tip Kalamata olives can be found, along with other Mediterranean olives, in tubs usually near the salad bar or deli section of most supermarkets. Sometimes they are available pitted, but to pit them yourself, place the olives on a work surface and lightly mash them by hitting with the side of a chef's knife with the heel of your hand. The pits are then easily removed.

Balsamic Greens Salad

Elaine Lenart, Plymouth, MI

"I never had to worry about my weight until I turned 50," writes Elaine. She quickly took care of her problem by joining Weight Watchers and losing 12 pounds. "My weight loss motivated several of my friends and family members to join and experience the same success I had," she says. Elaine often serves this salad as an opening for a dinner party or family gathering. You could add canned water-packed tuna or cubed cooked chicken to it to make it a main-dish lunch or light dinner.

3 tablespoons balsamic vinegar

1 tablespoon extra-virgin olive oil

1 garlic clove, minced

1 teaspoon Dijon mustard

1 teaspoon anchovy paste

1 (6-ounce) bag baby spinach leaves

½ (10-ounce) bag romaine lettuce, torn into bite-size pieces

1 tomato, chopped

½ cucumber, peeled, seeded, and chopped

½ red onion, thinly sliced

8 oil-cured black olives, pitted and chopped

¼ cup crumbled reduced-fat feta cheese

MAKES 6 SERVINGS

Whisk the vinegar, oil, garlic, mustard, and anchovy paste in a large bowl. Add the spinach, lettuce, tomato, cucumber, onion, olives, and cheese; gently toss to coat. Serve at once.

PER SERVING (generous 1¾ cups): 70 Cal, 4 g Fat, 1 g Sat Fat, 0 g Trans Fat, 2 mg Chol, 276 mg Sod, 6 g Carb, 2 g Fib, 3 g Prot, 59 mg Calc. **POINTS** value: **1**.

tip Anchovy paste is a puree of anchovies combined with vinegar and spices. It comes in tubes, making it convenient to use in sauces, dips, and dressings. Because anchovy paste is salty, use it sparingly. It will keep in the refrigerator for up to three months. If you don't care for the taste of anchovies, you can substitute ¼ teaspoon of salt.

SOUPS AND SALADS

ARUGULA WITH BASIL AND
OVEN-ROASTED TOMATOES

Arugula with Basil and Oven-Roasted Tomatoes

Ann Martinuzzi, Oakland Gardens, NY

Ann was inspired to lose weight when she learned she was to become a grandmother and wanted to be healthy and able to play with her grandchild. Her weight loss began that day in December 2000 and she has since lost a commendable 87 pounds. She has only 10 more pounds to lose before reaching her goal weight. Ann often serves this salad when she has Weight Watchers friends for lunch.

2 plum tomatoes

2 teaspoons plain dry bread crumbs

2 tablespoons balsamic vinegar

1 tablespoon extra-virgin olive oil

½ teaspoon salt

¼ teaspoon freshly ground pepper

1 (5-ounce) bag baby arugula

½ cup chopped fresh basil

2 tablespoons sliced almonds, toasted

MAKES 4 SERVINGS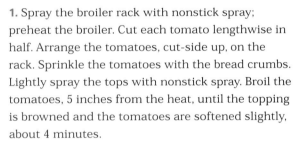

1. Spray the broiler rack with nonstick spray; preheat the broiler. Cut each tomato lengthwise in half. Arrange the tomatoes, cut-side up, on the rack. Sprinkle the tomatoes with the bread crumbs. Lightly spray the tops with nonstick spray. Broil the tomatoes, 5 inches from the heat, until the topping is browned and the tomatoes are softened slightly, about 4 minutes.

2. Whisk the vinegar, oil, salt, and pepper in a large bowl. Add the arugula, basil, and almonds; gently toss to coat. Serve with the tomatoes.

PER SERVING (1 cup salad with 1 tomato half): 73 Cal, 5 g Fat, 1 g Sat Fat, 0 g Trans Fat, 0 mg Chol, 315 mg Sod, 6 g Carb, 2 g Fib, 2 g Prot, 79 mg Calc. *POINTS* value: *1.*

Apple and Carrot Salad

Sharon F. Keefer, Cumberland, MD

Sharon, who lost over 26 pounds on the program, attends meetings with a friend—
a surefire way to keep on track. You can add cubes of cooked chicken, turkey, or ham
to this Waldorf-like salad for a quick and easy main-dish lunch or light dinner.

¼ cup fat-free mayonnaise

1 tablespoon cider vinegar

1 teaspoon sugar

2 Granny Smith apples,
  chopped

½ (10-ounce) bag matchstick-
  cut carrots (about 2 cups)

1 celery stalk, finely chopped

¼ cup raisins

1 tablespoon chopped
  toasted walnuts

2 slices bacon, cooked
  and crumbled

MAKES 4 SERVINGS

Combine the mayonnaise, vinegar, and sugar in a
large bowl. Add the apples, carrots, celery, raisins,
and walnuts; toss to coat well. Sprinkle with the
bacon and serve at once.

PER SERVING (1¼ cups): 134 Cal, 3 g Fat, 1 g Sat Fat,
0 g Trans Fat, 3 mg Chol, 183 mg Sod, 27 g Carb,
4 g Fib, 2 g Prot, 25 mg Calc. **POINTS** value: **2.**

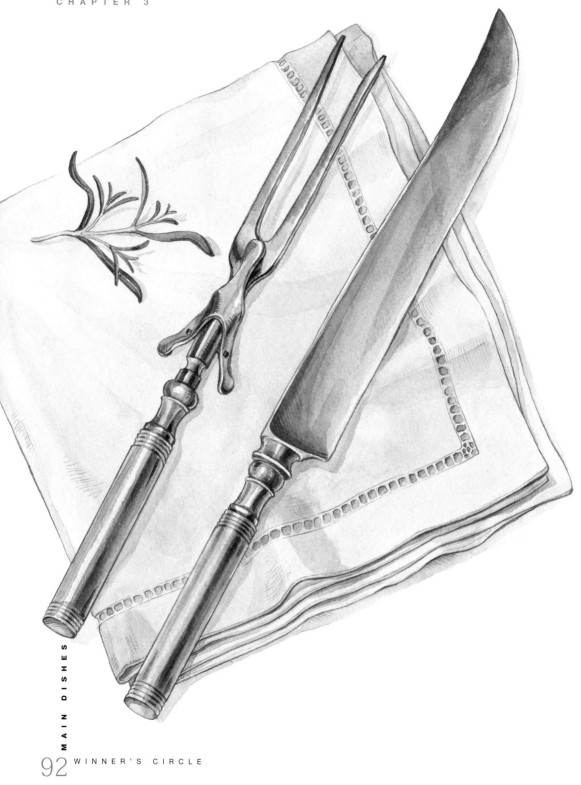

Main Dishes

MEAT, POULTRY, SEAFOOD, AND VEGETARIAN ENTRÉES

Greek-Style Cannelloni with Tomato-Mint Sauce **94**
Herb-Crusted Salmon with Roasted Asparagus Sauce **97**
Beef and Vegetable Stir-Fry **98**
Quick and Easy Sloppy Joe with Macaroni **100**
Cabbage Casserole **101**
Roasted Balsamic Pork Tenderloin **102**
Tart Apple Pork **103**
Roast Pork Tenderloin with Zucchini "Noodles" Alfredo **105**
Honey-Grilled Chicken with Asian Pear Chow-Chow **106**
Lemon Chicken with Artichokes and Spinach **108**
Stuffed Chicken Cordon Bleu **109**
Spinach and Cheese–Stuffed Chicken Breasts **111**
Tigue's Spicy Chicken and Shrimp Stir-Fry **112**
Jambalaya **114**
Chicken and Penne Casserole with Tomatoes and Goat Cheese **115**
Tuscan Pasta Toss **116**
Penne with Sausage and Broccoli **117**
Garlic and Herb–Stuffed Turkey Breast **119**
Roasted Salmon Florentine **120**
Salmon Loaf **122**
Tilapia Puttanesca **123**
Scallops Persillade **124**
Creamy Lemon Shrimp **125**
Garlic Pasta with Lemony Scallops and Tomatoes **127**
Greek Shrimp and Pasta **128**
East-Meets-West Shrimp Frittata **130**
Zucchini and Veggie Burger Pasta **131**
Fiesta Stuffed Peppers **132**
Veggie Taco Wraps **133**
Meatless Cheese Steak Pitas **135**
Vegetarian Chili **136**
Soft Tacos with Goat Cheese and Mango Salsa **137**
Veggie Enchiladas **138**
Roasted Spaghetti Squash with Garlic, Broccoli, and Tomatoes **140**
Roasted Vegetable Omelette **141**

Greek-Style Cannelloni with Tomato-Mint Sauce

Julie DeMatteo, Clementon, NJ

"I've recently acquired a passion for mint and I have been using it with abandon," says Julie. She added it to this traditional Italian dish and voilà: delicious success! If fresh mint isn't available, don't use dried; substitute fresh basil instead. Egg roll wrappers are a convenient, low-*POINTS* value way to make cannelloni.

2 teaspoons olive oil

2 garlic cloves, minced

2 cups marinara sauce

¼ cup chopped fresh mint

1 (10-ounce) package frozen chopped spinach, thawed and squeezed dry

1 cup fat-free ricotta cheese

¼ cup crumbled reduced-fat feta cheese

2 egg whites, lightly beaten

10 kalamata olives, pitted and chopped

½ teaspoon dried oregano

½ teaspoon pepper

¼ teaspoon cinnamon

6 (6-inch square) egg roll wrappers

6 (1-ounce) sticks part-skim mozzarella string cheese

2 tablespoons grated Parmesan cheese

MAKES 6 SERVINGS

1. Preheat the oven to 400°F. Spray a 9-inch square baking dish with nonstick spray.

2. Heat the oil in a medium nonstick saucepan over medium heat. Add the garlic and cook until golden, about 2 minutes. Add the sauce; bring to a boil. Remove from the heat and stir in the mint. Spread about ½ cup of the sauce on the bottom of the baking dish; set aside.

3. To make the cannelloni, combine the spinach, ricotta cheese, feta cheese, egg whites, olives, oregano, pepper, and cinnamon in a large bowl. Arrange the egg roll wrappers on a work surface. Spoon one-sixth of the spinach mixture across one wrapper. Top with 1 stick string cheese; roll up. Place seam-side down in the baking dish. Repeat with the remaining egg roll wrappers, spinach mixture, and string cheese. Spread the remaining 1½ cups sauce over the cannelloni. Bake, uncovered, until the filling is hot and the sauce is bubbly, about 30 minutes. Sprinkle with the Parmesan cheese and serve at once.

PER SERVING (1 cannelloni with ⅙ of the sauce): 273 Cal, 8 g Fat, 2 g Sat Fat, 0 g Trans Fat, 16 mg Chol, 956 mg Sod, 31 g Carb, 4 g Fib, 19 g Prot, 390 mg Calc. *POINTS* value: 5.

GREEK-STYLE CANNELLONI
WITH TOMATO-MINT SAUCE

HERB-CRUSTED SALMON
WITH ROASTED
ASPARAGUS SAUCE

Herb-Crusted Salmon with Roasted Asparagus Sauce

Virginia C. Anthony, Jacksonville, FL

Virginia's serving suggestion is to spoon some of the sauce on each serving plate, top with the salmon, then sprinkle with the asparagus tips.

1 pound fresh asparagus, trimmed

1 cup fat-free half-and-half

1 teaspoon Dijon mustard

2 teaspoons chopped fresh tarragon

1 teaspoon grated lemon zest

¾ teaspoon salt

¾ teaspoon freshly ground pepper

1½ slices firm white sandwich bread, made into crumbs (about ½ cup)

1 teaspoon chopped fresh dill

1 teaspoon chopped fresh chives

6 (4-ounce) center-cut salmon fillets

MAKES 6 SERVINGS

1. To make the asparagus sauce, preheat the oven to 450°F. Spray a nonstick baking sheet with nonstick spray. Arrange the asparagus on the sheet and bake, until the asparagus is crisp-tender, 8–10 minutes. Cut the tips off the asparagus and place in a small bowl. Cut the remaining asparagus into pieces and place in a food processor. With processor running, add the half-and-half through the feed tube; process until smooth. Transfer asparagus mixture to a medium saucepan and set over medium heat. Stir in mustard, 1 teaspoon of the tarragon, the lemon zest, ¼ teaspoon of the salt, and ¼ teaspoon of the pepper. Cook until heated through, about 3 minutes (do not boil). Keep warm.

2. Spray a baking sheet with nonstick spray. Combine the bread crumbs, dill, chives, and remaining 1 teaspoon tarragon in a bowl. Sprinkle the salmon with remaining salt and pepper. Top each fillet with one-sixth of crumb mixture; place on baking sheet. Lightly spray topping with nonstick spray. Bake until crust is browned and salmon is just opaque in center, about 15 minutes. Serve with sauce and asparagus tips.

PER SERVING (1 salmon fillet, ¼ cup sauce and ¼ cup asparagus tips): 198 Cal, 5 g Fat, 1 g Sat Fat, 0 g Trans Fat, 65 mg Chol, 466 mg Sod, 9 g Carb, 1 g Fib, 28 g Prot, 88 mg Calc. **POINTS** value: **4.**

MAIN DISHES

Beef and Vegetable Stir-Fry

Lisa Rundle, Gurnee, IL

What could be better, and better for you, than a plate full of this hearty stir-fry, chock-full of healthy, tasty vegetables? Lisa, who has lost 22 pounds on the program, likes to vary the vegetables she uses, sometimes using green or red bell peppers, snow peas, bok choy, or celery. "I look for flavor and color without adding to the total *POINTS* value," she writes. Your can also try this with chicken or shrimp.

½ cup low-sodium
    chicken broth

3 tablespoons reduced-sodium
    soy sauce

2 teaspoons cornstarch

1 teaspoon sugar

1 teaspoon Asian (dark)
    sesame oil

2 teaspoons canola oil

½ pound boneless sirloin steak,
    trimmed of all visible fat
    and cut into thin strips

1 onion, thinly sliced

½ pound fresh white
    mushrooms, thinly sliced

2 garlic cloves, minced

1 zucchini, sliced

1 yellow squash, sliced

3 cups shredded Chinese
    cabbage

1 cup bean sprouts

2 cups cooked brown rice

MAKES 4 SERVINGS

1. Combine the broth, soy sauce, cornstarch, sugar, and sesame oil in a small bowl; set aside.

2. Heat 1 teaspoon of the canola oil in a nonstick wok or a large, deep skillet over medium-high heat until a drop of water sizzles. Add the beef and stir-fry until cooked through, 2–3 minutes; transfer to a plate.

3. Add the remaining 1 teaspoon canola oil to the wok, then add the onion, mushrooms, and garlic. Stir-fry until softened, 4–5 minutes. Add the zucchini and yellow squash. Stir-fry until crisp-tender, 3–4 minutes. Add the cabbage and bean sprouts; stir-fry until the cabbage wilts and the bean sprouts are crisp-tender, 2–3 minutes. Add the broth mixture and cook, stirring constantly, until the mixture boils and thickens, about 1 minute. Add the beef and cook until heated through, about 1 minute. Serve over the rice.

PER SERVING (1 cup beef mixture with ½ cup rice): 287 Cal, 8 g Fat, 2 g Sat Fat, 0 g Trans Fat, 32 mg Chol, 536 mg Sod, 37 g Carb, 6 g Fib, 19 g Prot, 101 mg Calc. *POINTS* valuc: 6.

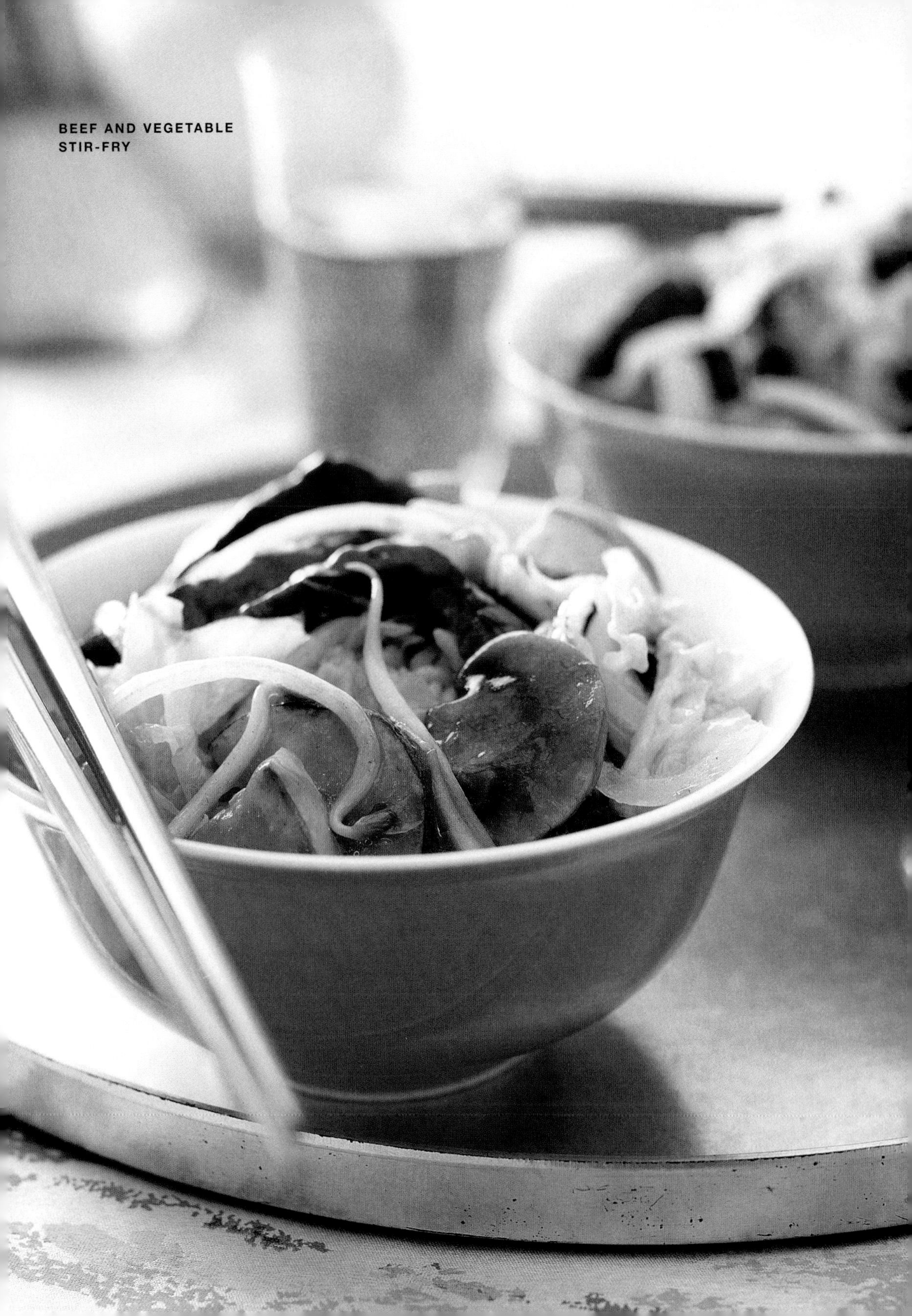

BEEF AND VEGETABLE
STIR-FRY

Quick and Easy Sloppy Joe with Macaroni

Eileen Pangoras, Absecon, NJ

Eileen has lost 9 pounds on Weight Watchers. She makes a nice change from the usual sloppy Joe served on a bun by stirring cooked macaroni into her spicy beef sauce. Chopped bell peppers help stretch the sauce without increasing the *POINTS* value. You could stretch it even further by also adding a chopped zucchini or yellow squash to the mixture. If you prefer, use ground turkey or chicken instead of beef.

1 cup elbow macaroni

2 teaspoons canola oil

1 green bell pepper, seeded and finely chopped

1 red bell pepper, seeded and finely chopped

1 onion, finely chopped

½ pound lean ground sirloin (10% or less fat)

1 (15½-ounce) can sloppy Joe sauce

MAKES 5 SERVINGS

1. Cook the macaroni according to package directions; drain and set aside.

2. Heat the oil in large nonstick skillet over medium-high heat. Add the bell peppers and onion; cook, stirring occasionally, until softened, about 8 minutes. Add the beef and cook, breaking it up with a wooden spoon, until the liquid evaporates and the beef begins to brown, about 6 minutes.

3. Stir in the macaroni and the sloppy Joe sauce; bring to a boil. Reduce the heat and simmer, uncovered, until the flavors are blended, about 3 minutes.

PER SERVING (1¼ cups): 329 Cal, 7 g Fat, 2 g Sat Fat, 0 g Trans Fat, 16 mg Chol, 1,149 mg Sod, 52 g Carb, 3 g Fib, 14 g Prot, 31 mg Calc. *POINTS* value: **7**.

tip To protect your nonstick cookware, invest in a wooden spoon or long-handled nonstick fork to use when breaking up clumps of ground meat.

Cabbage Casserole

Maud E. Woodsinger, Huntsville, AL

Want to make stuffed cabbage with half the fuss? Here's what Maud does: Instead of making rolls, she layers the ingredients for basic stuffed cabbage in a baking dish. It not only tastes like the real thing, but you save on prep time by not having to parboil, stuff, and roll cabbage leaves.

2 teaspoons canola oil

1 onion, finely chopped

1 green bell pepper, seeded and finely chopped

2 garlic cloves, minced

1 pound lean ground sirloin (10 % or less fat)

1 (14½-ounce) can diced tomatoes with mild green chiles

1 (8-ounce) can tomato sauce

½ cup cooked white rice

½ small head cabbage (about ¾ pound), shredded

MAKES 4 SERVINGS

1. Preheat the oven to 350°F. Spray a 9 x 13-inch baking dish with nonstick spray; set aside.

2. To make the filling, heat the oil in large nonstick skillet over medium-high heat. Add the onion, bell pepper, and garlic; cook, stirring occasionally, about 8 minutes. Add the beef and cook, breaking it up with a wooden spoon, until the liquid evaporates and the beef begins to brown, about 6 minutes. Stir in the diced tomatoes, tomato sauce, and rice; bring to a boil. Remove from the heat.

3. Spoon half of the filling in an even layer on the bottom of the baking dish. Top with all of the cabbage, then top with the remaining filling. Cover with foil and bake until the filling is hot and bubbly and the cabbage is very tender, about 1¼ hours.

PER SERVING (1¾ cups): 272 Cal, 11 g Fat, 3 g Sat Fat, 1 g Trans Fat, 32 mg Chol, 954 mg Sod, 24 g Carb, 5 g Fib, 21 g Prot, 105 mg Calc. *POINTS* value: **6.**

tip An ideal kitchen companion is a hand-held slicer called a mandoline. It's perfect for shredding cabbage, as well as slicing other vegetables.

Roasted Balsamic Pork Tenderloin

Jacqueline R. Ryan, Littleton, CO

Take care not to overcook this tender cut of meat. The balsamic marinade also works nicely with steak or chicken breast.

2 tablespoons balsamic
  vinegar
1 tablespoon extra-virgin
  olive oil
1 tablespoon chopped
  fresh thyme
2 teaspoons Dijon mustard
2 garlic cloves, minced
½ teaspoon freshly
  ground pepper
1 (1-pound) pork tenderloin,
  trimmed of all visible fat
2 shallots, minced
2 (5-ounce) bags baby
  spinach leaves
¼ teaspoon salt

MAKES 4 SERVINGS

1. Combine the vinegar, 2 teaspoons of the oil, the thyme, mustard, garlic, and pepper in a large zip-close plastic bag; add the pork. Squeeze out air and seal bag; turn to coat pork. Refrigerate at least 4 hours or up to 24 hours.

2. Preheat the oven to 475°F. Spray a small roasting pan with nonstick spray.

3. Remove the tenderloin from the marinade; discard the marinade. Spray a nonstick skillet with nonstick spray and set over medium-high heat. Add the pork and cook, turning occasionally, until browned, about 5 minutes. Transfer to the roasting pan. Roast until an instant-read thermometer inserted into the thickest part of the pork registers 160°F for medium, about 20–25 minutes. Transfer the pork to a carving board, let stand 10 minutes, then cut into 16 slices.

4. Meanwhile, heat the remaining 1 teaspoon oil in a nonstick skillet over medium-high heat. Add the shallots and cook until softened, about 2 minutes. Add spinach and salt, and cook, about 3–4 minutes. Serve with the pork.

PER SERVING (4 slices pork with ½ cup spinach): 198 Cal, 8 g Fat, 2 g Sat Fat, 0 g Trans Fat, 75 mg Chol, 287 mg Sod, 5 g Carb, 2 g Fib, 27 g Prot, 84 mg Calc. *POINTS* value: 4.

Tart Apple Pork

Cindy L. Woodall, Crawfordsville, IN

"My husband complains that pork loin has no taste and is dry, but since it's a lean meat, I always reach for it," says Cindy, who met this challenge with great success. Apples and fresh herbs complement the pork, giving it the moisture and flavor her husband wants. He loves this dish served with sweet potatoes; Cindy prefers rice. Either way, it's delicious.

4 (4-ounce) boneless center-cut pork loin chops, trimmed of all visible fat

1 tablespoon chopped fresh rosemary

1 tablespoon chopped fresh thyme

½ teaspoon salt

½ teaspoon freshly ground pepper

2 teaspoons canola oil

2 Granny Smith apples, peeled, cored, and sliced

1 large onion, thinly sliced

⅔ cup unsweetened apple juice

2 tablespoons honey mustard

MAKES 4 SERVINGS

1. Sprinkle the chops with the rosemary, thyme, salt, and pepper. Heat 1 teaspoon of the oil in a large nonstick skillet over medium-high heat. Add the chops and cook until browned and cooked through, 4–5 minutes on each side; transfer to a plate and cover to keep warm.

2. Heat the remaining 1 teaspoon oil in the same skillet over medium heat. Add the apples and onion. Cook, stirring occasionally, until tender and golden, about 8 minutes. Stir in the apple juice and honey mustard; bring to a boil. Reduce the heat and simmer, uncovered, until the sauce thickens slightly, about 5 minutes. Return chops to pan and cook, turning once, to heat through, about 2 minutes.

PER SERVING (1 chop with ½ cup apple mixture): 273 Cal, 11 g Fat, 3 g Sat Fat, 0 g Trans Fat, 67 mg Chol, 360 mg Sod, 21 g Carb, 2 g Fib, 24 g Prot, 36 mg Calc. *POINTS* value: **6.**

MAIN DISHES

ROAST PORK TENDERLOIN
WITH ZUCCHINI
"NOODLES" ALFREDO

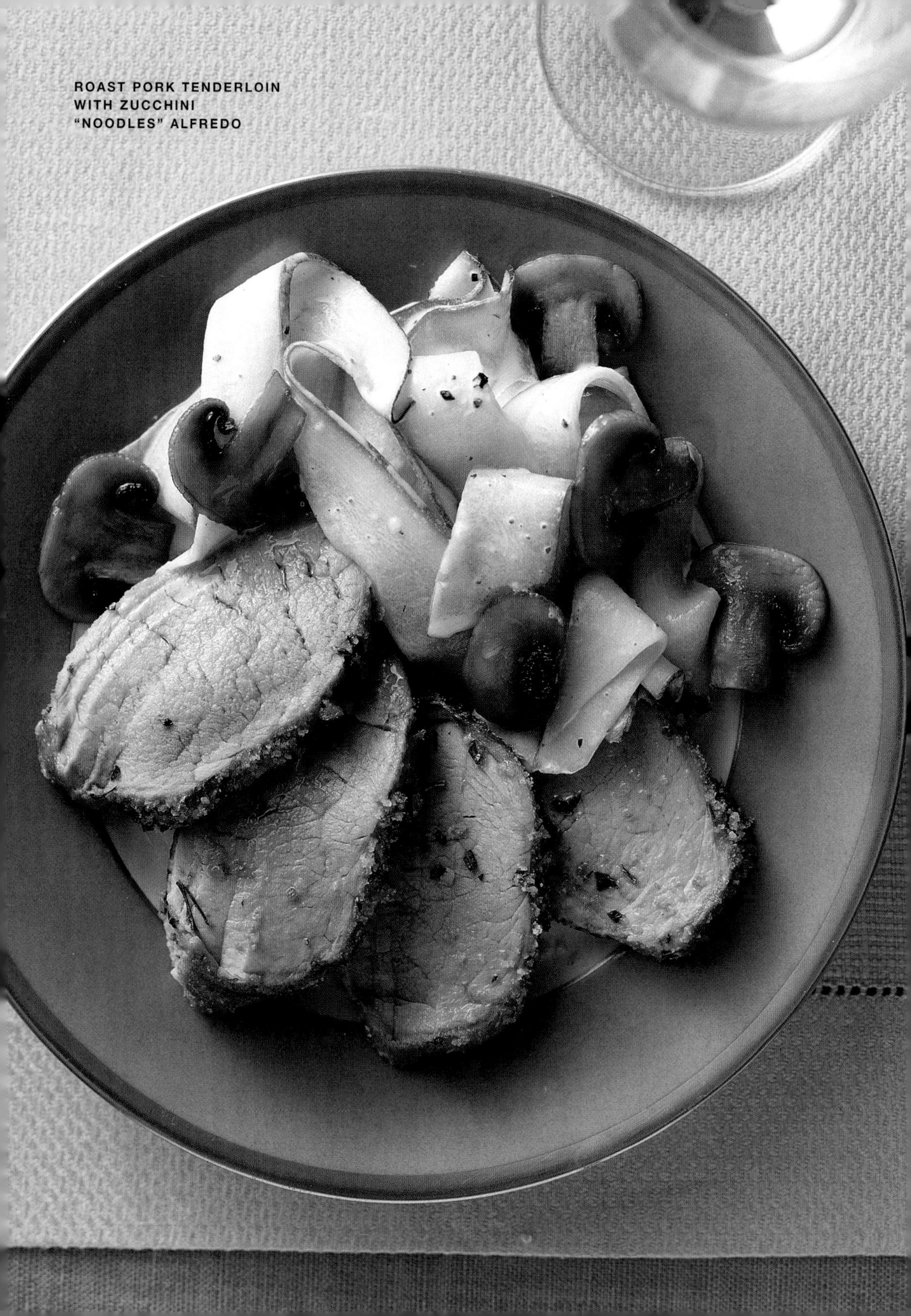

Roast Pork Tenderloin with Zucchini "Noodles" Alfredo

Anne Kern, Spring Valley, NY

Anne shares with us her clever trick for making noodles with a **POINTS** value of zero—a vegetable peeler used to shave zucchini into wide strips, resembling fettuccine.

1 tablespoon plain dry
bread crumbs

1 tablespoon chopped
fresh parsley

2 teaspoons chopped
fresh rosemary

2 teaspoons extra-virgin
olive oil

1 garlic clove, minced

¼ teaspoon salt

1 (1-pound) pork tenderloin,
trimmed of all visible fat

2 medium zucchini

½ pound fresh white
mushrooms, thinly sliced

¼ cup dry white wine

2 tablespoons fat-free
half-and-half

¼ teaspoon freshly
ground pepper

Pinch nutmeg

MAKES 4 SERVINGS

1. Preheat the oven to 450°F. Spray a small roasting pan with nonstick spray.

2. Combine the bread crumbs, parsley, rosemary, 1 teaspoon of the oil, the garlic, and salt in a small bowl. Rub the mixture all over the pork. Place the pork in the pan and roast until the topping is browned and an instant-read thermometer inserted into the thickest part of the pork registers 160°F for medium, 20–25 minutes. Transfer the pork to a carving board, let stand 10 minutes, then cut into about 16 slices.

3. Meanwhile, make shavings from the zucchini by running a vegetable peeler lengthwise down the zucchini. Heat the remaining 1 teaspoon oil in a large nonstick skillet over medium-high heat. Add the mushrooms and cook until browned, about 5 minutes. Add the zucchini and cook, stirring gently, until the zucchini just begins to soften, about 3 minutes. Stir in the wine, half-and-half, pepper, and nutmeg; bring to a boil. Reduce the heat and simmer, uncovered, until the flavors are blended and vegetables are tender, about 3 minutes. Serve with the pork.

PER SERVING (4 slices pork with generous ½ cup vegetable mixture): 212 Cal, 8 g Fat, 2 g Sat Fat, 0 g Trans Fat, 75 mg Chol, 224 mg Sod, 8 g Carb, 2 g Fib, 28 g Prot, 40 mg Calc. **POINTS** value: **5.**

Honey-Grilled Chicken with Asian Pear Chow-Chow

Janice Elder, Charlotte, NC

Janice has lost 20 pounds and finds her Weight Watchers meetings "supportive and fun." She typically serves this dish at dinner parties and "everyone asks for the recipe." The combination of Asian pears, sweet mango, and chopped dates is delicious. Asian pears are juicy, round, and crunchy with just a hint of sweetness. If you can't find them, use two ripe Bosc pears instead.

1 Asian pear, cored and diced

1 ripe mango, peeled
  and diced

2 tablespoons pitted
  chopped dates

2 tablespoons thinly sliced
  scallions

2 teaspoons grated lemon zest

3 tablespoons fresh
  lemon juice

2 tablespoons honey

¼ cup chopped fresh mint

½ teaspoon five-spice powder

½ teaspoon salt

¼ teaspoon freshly
  ground pepper

4 (5-ounce) skinless boneless
  chicken breasts

MAKES 4 SERVINGS

1. To make the chow-chow, combine the pear, mango, dates, scallions, zest, lemon juice, 1 tablespoon of the honey, and the mint in a large bowl. Cover and refrigerate until ready to serve, up to 2 days.

2. Combine the remaining 1 tablespoon honey with the five-spice powder, salt, and pepper in a small bowl. Rub the honey mixture on both sides of the chicken breasts.

3. Spray the grill rack with nonstick spray and prepare the grill, or spray a nonstick ridged grill pan with nonstick spray and set over medium-high heat. Place the chicken on the grill rack and cook until browned and cooked through, about 4 minutes on each side. Transfer the chicken to a cutting board; let stand 5 minutes before slicing on the diagonal. Serve with the chow-chow.

PER SERVING (1 chicken breast with 1 cup chow-chow): 254 Cal, 4 g Fat, 1 g Sat Fat, 0 g Trans Fat, 78 mg Chol, 363 mg Sod, 27 g Carb, 3 g Fib, 30 g Prot, 41 mg Calc. *POINTS* value: *5.*

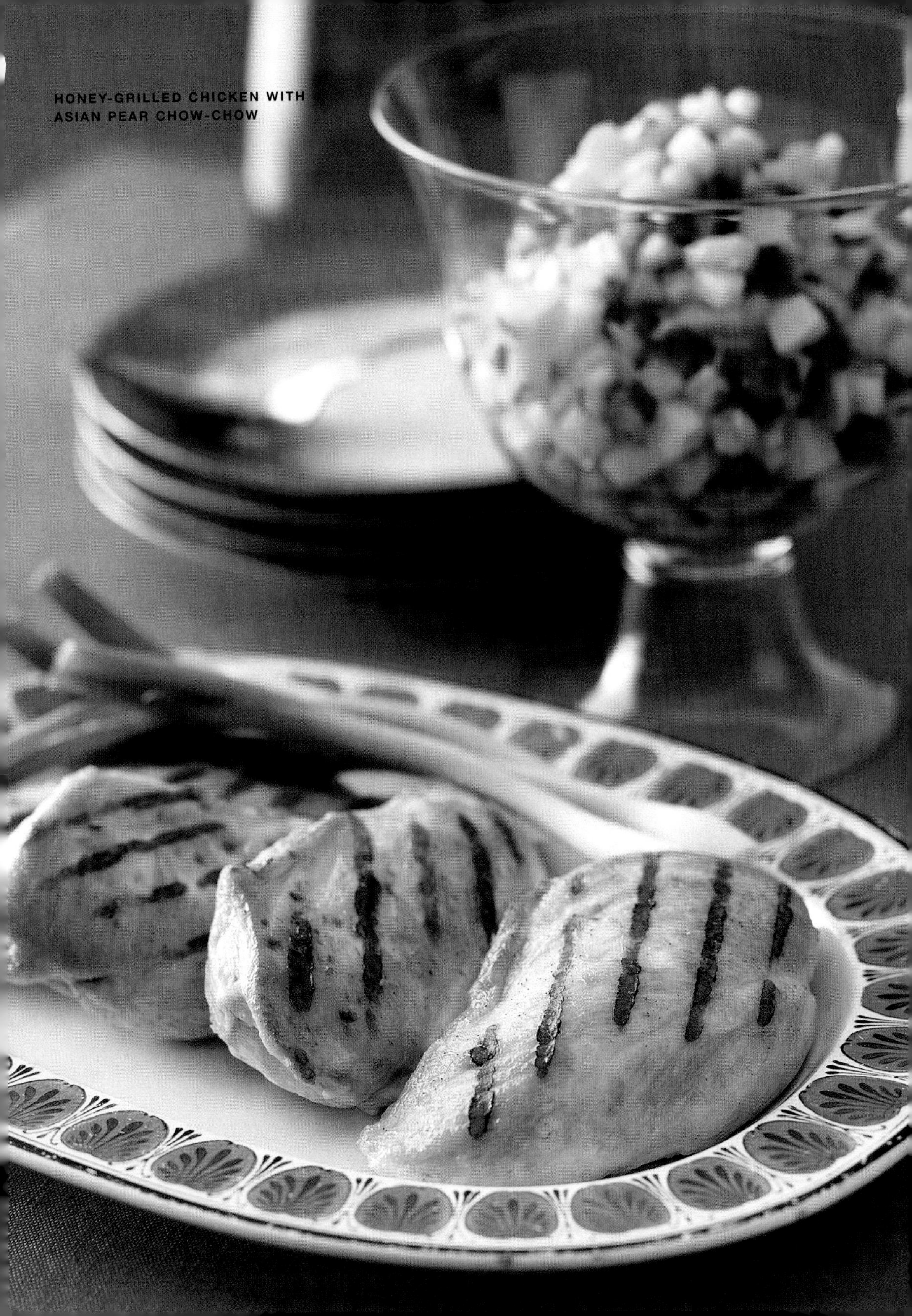

HONEY-GRILLED CHICKEN WITH ASIAN PEAR CHOW-CHOW

Lemon Chicken with Artichokes and Spinach

Lynda Douglas, Dorchester, MA

Lynda has lost an impressive 62 pounds on the Weight Watchers program. She likes the convenience of using pre-sliced mushrooms, canned artichokes, and triple-washed, ready-to-use spinach in this favorite skillet dinner. Serve with brown rice if you like—½ cup will increase the **POINTS** value by *2*.

¾ cup low-sodium chicken broth

2 teaspoons grated lemon zest

3 tablespoons fresh lemon juice

1 tablespoon cornstarch

1 teaspoon sugar

4 (5-ounce) skinless boneless chicken breasts

1 tablespoon chopped fresh dill

½ teaspoon salt

½ teaspoon freshly ground pepper

2 teaspoons olive oil

1 (8-ounce) package sliced fresh white mushrooms

1 (14-ounce) can artichoke hearts, drained and halved

1 (5-ounce) bag baby spinach leaves

1 tablespoon chopped capers

MAKES 4 SERVINGS

1. Combine the broth, zest, lemon juice, cornstarch, and sugar in a small bowl; set aside.

2. Sprinkle both sides of each chicken breast with the dill, salt, and pepper. Heat 1 teaspoon of the oil in a large nonstick skillet over medium-high heat. Add the chicken and cook until browned and almost cooked through, about 3 minutes on each side. Transfer to a plate; keep warm.

3. Heat the remaining 1 teaspoon oil in same skillet. Add mushrooms and cook until browned, about 6 minutes. Add the artichoke hearts and spinach and cook, stirring often, until the spinach is wilted, about 2 minutes. Add the broth mixture and cook, stirring constantly, until the mixture boils and thickens, about 1 minute. Add the chicken and capers and cook until heated through, about 1 minute.

PER SERVING (1 chicken breast with ¾ cup vegetable mixture): 224 Cal, 5 g Fat, 1 g Sat Fat, 0 g Trans Fat, 81 mg Chol, 631 mg Sod, 10 g Carb, 2 g Fib, 33 g Prot, 103 mg Calc. **POINTS** value: **4**.

tip One medium lemon yields 2 to 3 tablespoons juice and 2 to 3 teaspoons zest.

Stuffed Chicken Cordon Bleu

Teri Peterson, Pinehurst, NC

This classic chicken dish is truly special and worth the effort of every step.

1 onion, finely chopped

1 cup thinly sliced fresh
  white mushrooms

1 (6-ounce) package baby
  spinach leaves

2 tablespoons crumbled
  reduced-fat goat cheese

5 tablespoons plain dry
  bread crumbs

2 egg whites, lightly beaten

2 teaspoons cold water

4 (5-ounce) skinless boneless
  chicken breasts

2 (1-ounce) slices reduced-fat
  Swiss cheese, each cut
  in half

4 thin slices turkey ham

MAKES 4 SERVINGS

1. Preheat the oven to 425°F. Spray a nonstick baking pan with nonstick spray. To make the filling, spray a nonstick skillet with nonstick spray and set over medium-high heat. Add the onion and mushrooms; cook, until softened, about 5 minutes. Add the spinach and cook, 3–4 minutes. Remove the skillet from the heat. Stir in the goat cheese and 1 tablespoon of the bread crumbs; set aside.

2. Whisk egg whites with the water in a small bowl. Place the remaining $\frac{1}{4}$ cup bread crumbs in another small bowl.

3. Cut a pocket into the side of each chicken breast about $2\frac{1}{2}$-inches long. Place one-quarter of filling inside each slit. Lightly press pocket closed. Wrap 1 half slice of cheese, then one slice of ham around each chicken breast, making sure the ham covers the cheese; secure with a toothpick. Dip the chicken, one piece at a time, into the egg white mixture, then into the bread crumbs. Transfer to the baking pan. Lightly spray the chicken with nonstick spray. Bake until the chicken is cooked through, about 25 minutes. Remove the toothpicks before serving.

PER SERVING (1 chicken breast): 303 Cal, 9 g Fat, 4 g Sat Fat, 0 g Trans Fat, 98 mg Chol, 431 mg Sod, 14 g Carb, 2 g Fib, 41 g Prot, 240 mg Calc. *POINTS* value: **6.**

MAIN DISHES

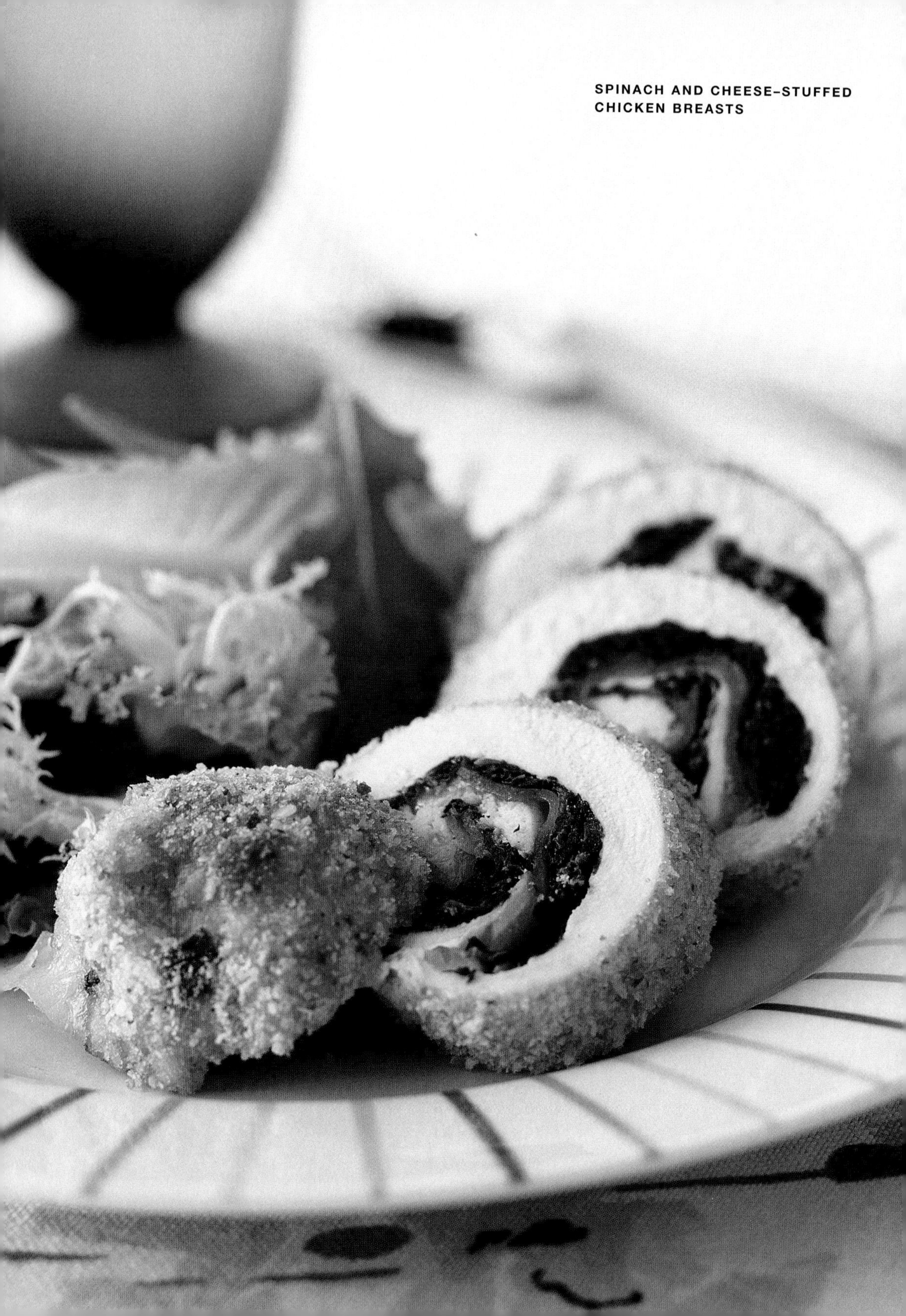

SPINACH AND CHEESE-STUFFED CHICKEN BREASTS

Spinach and Cheese–Stuffed Chicken Breasts

Heather M.K. Smith, Moscow, ID

Heather is a graduate student who has gained 40 pounds in the past six years. Since joining Weight Watchers, she has lost nine pounds towards her goal. She enjoys cooking this dish on weekends with a friend—they love the taste of the spinach, cheese, and turkey pepperoni stuffing. Turkey pepperoni has plenty of flavor and little fat. It comes in packages of small, thin slices, perfect for this recipe, or as a topping for pizza.

2 egg whites, lightly beaten

2 teaspoons cold water

¼ cup plain dry bread crumbs

4 (5-ounce) skinless boneless chicken breasts

1 (10-ounce) package frozen chopped spinach, thawed and squeezed dry

2 (1-ounce) slices reduced-fat Swiss cheese, each cut in half

2 ounces (from a 6-ounce package) thinly sliced, ready-to-eat turkey pepperoni (about 16 slices)

MAKES 4 SERVINGS

1. Preheat the oven to 425°F. Spray a nonstick baking sheet with nonstick spray.

2. Whisk together the egg whites with the water in a small bowl. Place the bread crumbs in another small bowl.

3. Lightly pound the chicken between 2 sheets of wax paper with a mallet or rolling pin to ¼-inch thickness. Top each chicken breast with one-quarter of the spinach, 1 half slice of cheese, and 4 slices of pepperoni. Roll up each chicken breast from a short side.

4. Dip the chicken, one piece at a time, into the egg white mixture, then into the bread crumbs. Place the chicken, seam-side down, on the baking sheet.

5. Spray the tops of the chicken lightly with nonstick spray. Bake until the chicken is cooked through and the crust is golden, about 25 minutes. Cut each roll into 4 or 5 slices.

PER SERVING (1 chicken roll): 287 Cal, 9 g Fat, 4 g Sat Fat, 0 g Trans Fat, 105 mg Chol, 547 mg Sod, 9 g Carb, 2 g Fib, 41 g Prot, 233 mg Calc.
POINTS value: 6.

Tigue's Spicy Chicken and Shrimp Stir-Fry

Suzanne Tigue Shore, Surprise, AZ

Suzanne has lost over 41 pounds on the program so far and is inspired to reach her goal all the more after winning Honorable Mention for this delicious stir-fry. "My husband requests it all the time," says Suzanne, who serves it often. Rice stick noodles, which need only softening in hot water, keep the recipe easy.

2 ounces rice stick noodles

½ cup low-sodium
   chicken broth

1 tablespoon reduced-sodium
   soy sauce

1 tablespoon cornstarch

1 teaspoon Thai fish sauce

½ teaspoon dark sesame oil

¼ teaspoon crushed red pepper

1 tablespoon canola oil

1 (5-ounce) skinless boneless
   chicken breast, cut into strips

3 scallions, thinly sliced

1 tablespoon minced peeled
   fresh ginger

2 garlic cloves, minced

1 medium zucchini, sliced

½ (10-ounce) bag matchstick-
   cut carrots (1 cup)

¼ pound snow peas, halved

1 (8-ounce) package frozen
   cooked salad shrimp, thawed

MAKES 4 SERVINGS

1. Bring a medium pot of water to a boil. Remove from the heat; add the noodles and soak until softened, 5–6 minutes. Drain and set aside.

2. Combine the broth, soy sauce, cornstarch, fish sauce, sesame oil, and crushed pepper in small bowl; set aside.

3. Heat the canola oil in a large nonstick wok or large, deep skillet over medium-high heat until a drop of water sizzles. Add chicken and stir-fry until cooked through, 2–3 minutes. Transfer the chicken to a bowl and set aside. Add the scallions, ginger, and garlic; stir-fry until fragrant, about 15 seconds. Add zucchini, carrots, and snow peas; stir-fry until crisp-tender, 3–4 minutes. Add the broth mixture and cook, stirring constantly, until the mixture boils and thickens, about 1 minute. Stir in the shrimp, chicken, and noodles. Cook, tossing frequently, until heated through, about 1 minute.

PER SERVING (1¼ cups): 218 Cal, 4 g Fat, 1 g Sat Fat, 0 g Trans Fat, 131 mg Chol, 442 mg Sod, 23 g Carb, 3 g Fib, 23 g Prot, 74 mg Calc. *POINTS* value: **4.**

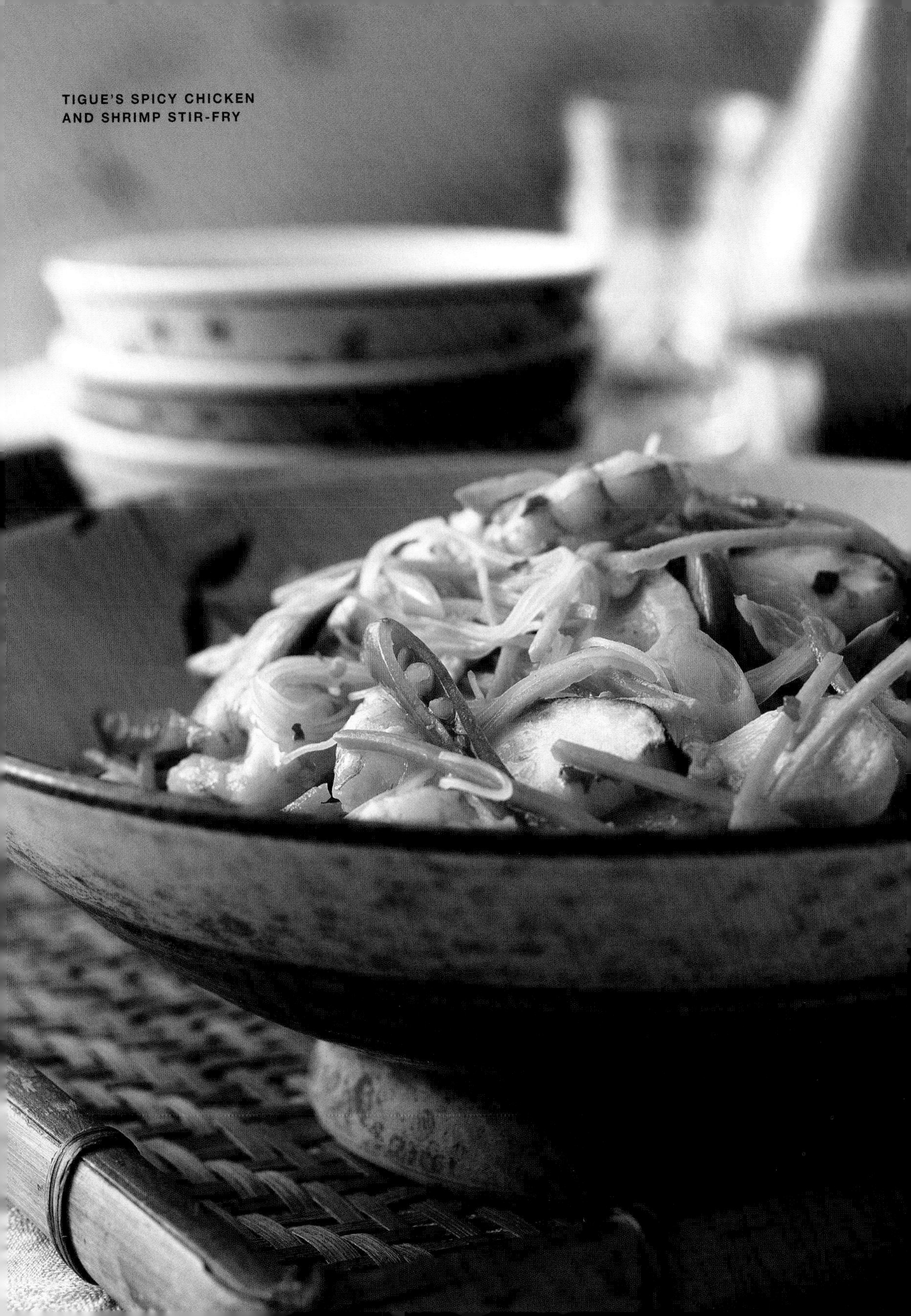

TIGUE'S SPICY CHICKEN AND SHRIMP STIR-FRY

Jambalaya

James C. Nestico, Willamsville, NY

Along with gumbo and crawfish pie, jambalaya is one of the famous dishes of Louisiana. There are many versions of this spicy Creole dish—using various combinations of chicken, ham, shrimp, sausage, pork, and even duck. The one common ingredient, however, is rice.

½ pound skinless boneless chicken breast, cut into ¼-inch slices

½ pound large shrimp, peeled and deveined

2 teaspoons Cajun seasoning

1 tablespoon olive oil

1 onion, chopped

1 green bell pepper, seeded and diced

1 red bell pepper, seeded and diced

1 celery stalk, diced

2 garlic cloves, minced

1 cup long-grain white rice

4 cups low-sodium chicken broth

1 (14½-ounce) can diced tomatoes

¼ teaspoon dried thyme

½ pound smoked turkey kielbasa, cut into ¼-inch-thick slices

MAKES 6 SERVINGS

1. Sprinkle the chicken and shrimp with the Cajun seasoning. Heat the oil in a large nonstick deep skillet over medium-high heat. Add the chicken and shrimp and cook, stirring occasionally, until the chicken is browned and the shrimp is just opaque in the center, about 4 minutes; transfer to a bowl.

2. Add the onion, bell peppers, celery, and garlic to the skillet. Cook over medium heat, stirring frequently, until tender, about 8 minutes. Stir in the rice; cook 1 minute. Add the broth, tomatoes, and thyme; bring to a boil. Reduce the heat, and simmer, covered, until the rice is tender, about 20 minutes. Add the chicken, shrimp, and kielbasa; cook until heated through, about 3 minutes.

PER SERVING (1½ cups): 325 Cal, 8 g Fat, 2 g Sat Fat, 0 g Trans Fat, 104 mg Chol, 611 mg Sod, 38 g Carb, 3 g Fib, 25 g Prot, 65 mg Calc. *POINTS* value: **7.**

Chicken and Penne Casserole with Tomatoes and Goat Cheese

Pat Daigle, Groves, TX

Like many of us, Pat and her sister get tired of their recipes and find it hard to come up with new ones. So in the spirit of sharing something good that she has created (which is what this book is all about), Pat gives us this hearty and satisfying dish. She developed it for her sister, who loves chicken.

2 cups penne pasta

2 teaspoons olive oil

3 cups sliced fresh white mushrooms

1 onion, chopped

2 tomatoes, chopped

1 cup cubed cooked skinless chicken breast

1 cup black beans, rinsed and drained

½ cup fat-free egg substitute

¼ cup low-sodium chicken broth

2 ounces reduced-fat goat cheese, crumbled

2 tablespoons plain dry bread crumbs

1 tablespoon grated Parmesan cheese

1 tablespoon chopped fresh parsley

MAKES 6 SERVINGS

1. Preheat the oven to 375°F. Spray a 7 x 11-inch baking dish with nonstick spray.

2. Cook the pasta according to package directions; drain. Transfer to a large bowl.

3. Heat 1 teaspoon of the oil in a large nonstick skillet over medium-high heat. Add the mushrooms and onion; cook, stirring frequently, until softened, about 8 minutes. Add the mushroom mixture to the pasta in the bowl. Stir in the tomatoes, chicken, beans, egg substitute, and broth. Spoon the mixture into the baking dish. Top with the goat cheese.

4. Combine the bread crumbs, Parmesan cheese, and parsley with the remaining 1 teaspoon oil in a small bowl. Sprinkle the crumb mixture over the casserole. Bake, uncovered, until the topping is browned and the filling is hot and bubbly, about 40 minutes.

PER SERVING (1 cup): 250 Cal, 5 g Fat, 1 g Sat Fat, 0 g Trans Fat, 23 mg Chol, 282 mg Sod, 33 g Carb, 5 g Fib, 18 g Prot, 56 mg Calc. *POINTS* value: 5.

MAIN DISHES

Tuscan Pasta Toss

Angela Jones, Huntington, WV

Angela finds the Weight Watchers At Work meetings that she attends "very encouraging" and she has lost upwards of 18 pounds. She created this main-dish salad when challenged by her husband to create dinner using items from their pantry. "After the first bite we knew we had a winner," she writes. Served warm or cold, it's ideal for a summer luncheon or quick weeknight supper. On special occasions, Angela often drizzles a little white truffle oil over the dish.

½ (16-ounce) box farfalle
   (bowtie pasta)
1 (14-ounce) can artichoke
   hearts, drained and
   coarsely chopped
1 cup cooked sliced skinless
   chicken breast
1 cup frozen peas, thawed
¼ cup sliced pimientos
¼ cup chopped fresh basil
6 oil-packed sun-dried
   tomatoes, drained, patted
   dry with paper towels,
   and chopped
1 tablespoon extra-virgin
   olive oil
½ teaspoon freshly
   ground pepper
2 ounces reduced-fat feta
   cheese, crumbled

MAKES 4 SERVINGS

1. Cook the farfalle according to package directions; drain. Rinse under cold running water. Transfer the farfalle to a large bowl.

2. Add the artichoke hearts, chicken, peas, pimientos, basil, sun-dried tomatoes, oil, and pepper; toss to coat. Sprinkle with the feta cheese.

PER SERVING (1¼ cups): 396 Cal, 8 g Fat, 2 g Sat Fat, 0 g Trans Fat, 35 mg Chol, 698 mg Sod, 56 g Carb, 7 g Fib, 26 g Prot, 58 mg Calc. *POINTS* value: **8.**

tip You can make this vegetarian by omitting the chicken and adding rinsed and drained canned chickpeas (garbanzo beans).

Penne with Sausage and Broccoli

Alvera C. Butler, Columbia, SC

Alvera keeps this Italian family favorite easy by using frozen broccoli, but if you like, you can substitute fresh broccoli florets or chopped fresh broccoli rabe and add a little crushed red pepper to add a little heat.

½ pound sweet Italian turkey sausage links

1 tablespoon olive oil

1 onion, chopped

1 cup sliced fresh white mushrooms

1 (14½-ounce) can diced tomatoes

1 (10-ounce) box frozen broccoli florets, thawed

1 yellow squash, diced

2 cups cooked penne pasta

3 tablespoons grated Parmesan cheese

2 tablespoons chopped fresh basil

MAKES 4 SERVINGS

1. Spray a large nonstick deep skillet with nonstick spray and set over medium-high heat. Add the sausage and cook until browned on all sides and cooked through, about 15 minutes. Transfer the sausage to a plate. When the sausage is cool enough to handle, cut into ½-inch-thick slices.

2. Heat the oil over medium-high heat in the same skillet. Add the onion and mushrooms; cook, stirring frequently, until softened, about 8 minutes. Add the tomatoes, broccoli, and yellow squash; bring to a boil. Reduce the heat and simmer, covered, until the flavors are developed and the vegetables are crisp-tender 6–7 minutes. Stir in the pasta and sausage. Sprinkle with the cheese and basil and serve at once.

PER SERVING (2 cups): 270 Cal, 9 g Fat, 2 g Sat Fat, 0 g Trans Fat, 38 mg Chol, 555 mg Sod, 33 g Carb, 6 g Fib, 18 g Prot, 111 mg Calc. **POINTS** value: **5.**

tip Use spring-loaded tongs to turn the sausage when cooking—avoid piercing the sausage with a fork as this will cause the juices to escape.

GARLIC AND HERB-STUFFED
TURKEY BREAST

Garlic and Herb–Stuffed Turkey Breast

Elaine Sutherland, New York, NY

"This recipe has special meaning for me," says Elaine. While studying in Florence, Italy, one of Elaine's teachers taught her how to make this delicious stuffed turkey breast, since she would be missing Thanksgiving at home. The recipe remains one of Elaine's favorites.

1 tablespoon chopped fresh rosemary

2 teaspoons chopped fresh sage

2 teaspoons chopped fresh parsley

1 tablespoon extra-virgin olive oil

½ teaspoon salt

¼ teaspoon freshly ground pepper

1 skinless boneless turkey breast half, about 1½ pounds

3 garlic cloves, minced

1 cup low-sodium chicken broth

1 cup dry white wine

3 whole garlic cloves

1 bay leaf

MAKES 4 SERVINGS

1. Combine rosemary, sage, parsley, 2 teaspoons of oil, the salt, and pepper in a small bowl. With a long, thin knife, split turkey in half horizontally without cutting all the way through. Open turkey like a book. Cover with plastic wrap and lightly pound to flatten slightly. Spread half the herb mixture and the minced garlic over the turkey. Roll up tightly from one long side. Tie with string at 1-inch intervals. Rub remaining herb mixture over the rolled breast.

2. Heat remaining 1 teaspoon oil in a large nonstick Dutch oven over medium-high heat. Add turkey and cook, about 8 minutes. Add broth, wine, whole garlic cloves, and bay leaf; bring to a boil. Reduce heat and simmer, covered, about 35 minutes. Transfer to cutting board. Let stand 10 minutes; cut into 8 slices.

3. Bring liquid in pot to a boil. Reduce heat and simmer, uncovered, until liquid is reduced by half, about 6 minutes. Discard garlic cloves and bay leaf. Serve with turkey.

PER SERVING (2 turkey slices and 2 tablespoons sauce): 229 Cal, 5 g Fat, 1 g Sat Fat, 0 g Trans Fat, 113 mg Chol, 389 mg Sod, 2 g Carb, 0 g Fib, 42 g Prot, 34 mg Calc. *POINTS* value: *5.*

MAIN DISHES

Roasted Salmon Florentine

Annette L. Ilonzeh, Grapevine, TX

Annette has lost 33 pounds so far and says: "It's the camaraderie and the feeling that I'm not in this alone that keeps me motivated in my weight loss journey." She says her husband doesn't complain when she serves plain, grilled fish and chicken, but "he was thrilled when I first served this tasty salmon." Annette likes the taste too, but also likes the convenience of cooking in foil packets, which keeps the salmon tender and moist, and clean up a breeze.

1 cup chopped fresh spinach

½ (14-ounce) can artichoke hearts, drained and coarsely chopped

4 scallions, finely chopped

1 tablespoon capers

8 pitted black olives, sliced

3 garlic cloves, minced

2 teaspoons extra-virgin olive oil

1 (1¼-pound) salmon fillet

½ teaspoon salt

¼ teaspoon freshly ground pepper

MAKES 6 SERVINGS

1. Combine the spinach, artichoke hearts, chopped scallions, capers, olives, garlic, and oil in a large bowl; set aside.

2. Preheat the oven to 400°F. Spray a 12 x 18-inch foil rectangle with nonstick spray. Place the salmon on the foil and sprinkle with the salt and pepper. Arrange the spinach mixture over the salmon. Fold the foil over the salmon to make a packet, making a tight seal.

3. Place the packet on a baking sheet and roast until the salmon is just opaque in the center, 30–35 minutes. Open the ends of the foil packet first to allow steam to escape, then open the top of the foil packet. Serve drizzled with any juices.

PER SERVING (⅙ of salmon fillet with topping): 166 Cal, 6 g Fat, 1 g Sat Fat, 0 g Trans Fat, 54 mg Chol, 536 mg Sod, 4 g Carb, 1 g Fib, 22 g Prot, 30 mg Calc. *POINTS* value: **4**.

tip Other types of fish that would work well here are cod, orange roughy, or flounder fillets.

ROASTED SALMON
FLORENTINE

Salmon Loaf

Lee Baxter, Concord, CA

Sautéed onion and mushrooms keep this comforting, old-fashioned loaf moist, as well as adding flavor. For variety, use chopped shiitake mushrooms in place of white mushrooms. For added color and flavor, stir some shredded carrots or zucchini into the mixture.

3 slices firm white sandwich bread, torn

¼ cup fat-free milk

2 teaspoons canola oil

½ pound fresh white mushrooms, finely chopped

1 onion, finely chopped

¼ teaspoon salt

Pinch cayenne

2 (14¾-ounce) cans salmon, drained

¼ cup plain dry bread crumbs

2 egg whites, lightly beaten

MAKES 6 SERVINGS

1. Preheat the oven to 350°F. Spray a 5 x 9-inch loaf pan with nonstick spray.

2. Combine the bread and milk in a large bowl; let stand 10 minutes.

3. Heat the oil in a large nonstick skillet over medium-high heat. Add the mushrooms, onion, salt, and cayenne. Cook, stirring frequently, until browned, about 8 minutes.

4. Add the mushroom mixture, salmon, bread crumbs, and egg whites to the bread mixture; mix with a fork until blended. Spoon the mixture into the loaf pan; spread until even and smooth. Bake until the filling is hot and the topping is lightly browned, 50–55 minutes. Let stand 10 minutes, then cut into 6 slices.

PER SERVING (1 slice): 252 Cal, 11 g Fat, 2 g Sat Fat, 0 g Trans Fat, 71 mg Chol, 705 mg Sod, 14 g Carb, 1 g Fib, 26 g Prot, 218 mg Calc. *POINTS* value: **6**.

tip Remove the skin from the canned salmon, but not the soft, edible bones. Simply mash them with the salmon, using a fork—they're a great source of calcium.

Tilapia Puttanesca

Joan Emmanuel, Baldwin, NY

"I was trying to find something everyone in my house would eat. My nine-year-old loves any type of olive. My husband only wants pasta with sauce. For me, it's fish," writes Joan. This super fast tomato sauce, with bold flavor from capers and olives, served over fish fillets is her answer. Cod, haddock, grouper, and Chilean sea bass fillets are suitable alternatives to the tilapia. You can serve with your favorite pasta (1 cup cooked pasta will increase the *POINTS* value by 4).

2 teaspoons olive oil

4 (4-ounce) tilapia fillets

1 onion, finely chopped

3 garlic cloves, minced

1 cup canned Italian
peeled tomatoes

¼ cup dry white wine

3 tablespoons capers

10 oil-cured black olives,
pitted and chopped

¼ teaspoon crushed red pepper

¼ cup chopped fresh basil

MAKES 4 SERVINGS

1. Heat 1 teaspoon of the oil in a large nonstick skillet over medium-high heat. Add the fish and cook until lightly browned, about 2 minutes on each side. Transfer to a plate; set aside.

2. Heat the remaining 1 teaspoon oil in the same skillet over medium heat. Add the onion and garlic; cook, stirring frequently, until softened, about 8 minutes. Add the tomatoes, wine, capers, olives, and crushed red pepper; bring to a boil. Stir in the basil. Return the fish to the skillet. Reduce the heat and simmer, uncovered, until the fish is just opaque in the center, about 3 minutes.

PER SERVING (1 fish fillet with ⅓ cup sauce):
148 Cal, 6 g Fat, 1 g Sat Fat, 0 g Trans Fat, 41 mg Chol, 486 mg Sod, 8 g Carb, 2 g Fib, 17 g Prot, 40 mg Calc.
POINTS value: **3.**

Scallops Persillade

Marge Dix, San Antonio, TX

When entertaining, Marge likes to serve these scallops in attractive baking shells. The tasty crumb coating could also be sprinkled on pieces of sole or flounder fillets, then baked in a 400°F oven for 10 to 12 minutes.

⅓ cup plain dry bread crumbs

1 tablespoon chopped
  fresh parsley

1 tablespoon minced
  fresh chives

1 tablespoon melted butter

2 teaspoons fresh lemon juice

1 garlic clove, minced

1 pound sea scallops
  (about 20)

MAKES 4 SERVINGS

1. Spray the broiler rack with nonstick spray; preheat broiler.

2. Combine the bread crumbs, parsley, chives, butter, lemon juice, and garlic in a zip-close plastic bag. Add the scallops, in batches, shaking the bag to coat. Arrange the scallops in one layer on the broiler rack. Lightly spray the scallops with nonstick spray.

3. Broil, 4 inches from the heat, turning at least once, until the scallops are browned on the outside and just opaque in the center, 3–4 minutes.

PER SERVING (about 5 scallops): 184 Cal, 4 g Fat, 2 g Sat Fat, 0 g Trans Fat, 63 mg Chol, 341 mg Sod, 9 g Carb, 0 g Fib, 24 g Prot, 45 mg Calc. **POINTS** value: 4.

tip Scallops often come with tabs of muscle still attached to them. The muscle is tough and should be removed before cooking. To remove, simply peel the muscle tab away from the scallop and discard.

Creamy Lemon Shrimp

Tim Abernathy, Olathe, KS

Similar to a carbonara sauce but with shrimp and mushrooms instead of bacon, and fat-free milk instead of cream, Tim recreates a dish from his past. "Before my wife and I joined Weight Watchers," he writes, "a restaurant we frequented served this dish loaded with cream and butter. After many tries, we came up with a way to still enjoy our favorite recipe without all the calories and fat."

4 ounces linguine

1 cup fat-free milk

¼ cup fat-free egg substitute

2 tablespoons fresh
    lemon juice

1 tablespoon cornstarch

½ teaspoon salt

¼ teaspoon dry mustard

1 tablespoon olive oil

½ pound fresh white
    mushrooms, thinly sliced

½ pound cooked, peeled,
    large shrimp

1 (14-ounce) can artichoke
    hearts, drained and
    coarsely chopped

MAKES 6 SERVINGS

1. Cook the linguine according to package directions; drain.

2. Combine the milk, egg substitute, lemon juice, cornstarch, salt, and mustard in a small bowl; set aside.

3. Heat the oil in a large nonstick skillet over medium-high heat. Add the mushrooms and cook, stirring frequently, until browned, about 5 minutes.

4. Add the milk mixture and cook over low heat, stirring constantly, until the mixture just comes to a simmer. Stir in the linguine, shrimp, and artichoke hearts. Reduce the heat and simmer, uncovered, tossing to coat, until the flavors are blended and the sauce thickens slightly, about 3 minutes.

PER SERVING (1 cup): 177 Cal, 3 g Fat, 1 g Sat Fat, 0 g Trans Fat, 57 mg Chol, 590 mg Sod, 24 g Carb, 3 g Fib, 14 g Prot, 72 mg Calc. *POINTS* value: **3**.

GARLIC PASTA WITH
LEMONY SCALLOPS AND
TOMATOES

Garlic Pasta with Lemony Scallops and Tomatoes

Claudette Bruschuk, Lake Bluff, IL

Claudette made this for her husband's family and "they just raved about how great it tasted, not knowing it was a low-calorie dish." Sometimes she uses half shrimp and half scallops and, when available, grape tomatoes, which are smaller and quite a bit sweeter than cherry tomatoes.

8 ounces linguine

2 teaspoons olive oil

1 pound sea scallops (about 20)

1 pint grape tomatoes or cherry tomatoes, each cut in half

2 garlic cloves, minced

½ teaspoon salt

¼ teaspoon crushed red pepper

¼ cup sliced fresh basil

2 tablespoons fresh lemon juice

MAKES 6 SERVINGS

1. Cook the linguine according to package directions; drain.

2. Heat 1 teaspoon of the oil in a large nonstick skillet over medium-high heat. Add the scallops and cook, turning at least once, until browned on the outside and just opaque in the center, 3–4 minutes. Transfer the scallops to a plate.

3. Heat the remaining 1 teaspoon oil in the same skillet over medium-high heat. Add the tomatoes, garlic, salt, and crushed red pepper. Cook, stirring frequently, until the tomatoes begin to soften, about 5 minutes. Add the linguine and scallops; heat through. Remove from the heat and stir in the basil and lemon juice. Serve at once.

PER SERVING (1 cup): 244 Cal, 3 g Fat, 0 g Sat Fat, 0 g Trans Fat, 37 mg Chol, 376 mg Sod, 32 g Carb, 2 g Fib, 20 g Prot, 29 mg Calc. *POINTS* value: **5**.

tip If you have ripe regular tomatoes on hand, you can chop and use them, or even a 14½-ounce can of diced tomatoes would be fine instead of the grape tomatoes.

MAIN DISHES

Greek Shrimp and Pasta

James C. Nestico, Williamsville, NY

James deliciously combined these everyday Mediterranean ingredients to create a tantalizingly fragrant dish that tempts everyone in the house to the kitchen. It's hard to resist eating every bit of it hot, but cold leftovers are also yummy.

8 ounces penne

1 tablespoon olive oil

1 onion, finely chopped

2 garlic cloves, minced

½ pound large shrimp, peeled and deveined

4 plum tomatoes, diced

15 oil-cured black olives, pitted and chopped

1 (8-ounce) bottle clam juice

¼ cup crumbled reduced-fat feta cheese

3 tablespoons chopped fresh oregano

MAKES 6 SERVINGS

1. Cook penne according to package directions; drain.

2. Heat the oil in a large nonstick skillet over medium-high heat. Add the onion and garlic; cook, stirring frequently, until softened, about 5 minutes. Add the shrimp and cook, stirring occasionally, until the shrimp are just opaque in the center, about 3 minutes.

3. Add the tomatoes and olives; cook, stirring occasionally, until softened, about 3 minutes.

4. Add the clam juice; bring to a boil. Stir in the penne, cheese, and oregano. Reduce the heat and simmer, tossing well, until the flavors are blended and the cheese just begins to melt, about 1 minute.

PER SERVING (1⅓ cups): 236 Cal, 6 g Fat, 1 g Sat Fat, 0 g Trans Fat, 59 mg Chol, 366 mg Sod, 32 g Carb, 3 g Fib, 13 g Prot, 53 mg Calc. *POINTS* value: 5.

GREEK SHRIMP AND PASTA

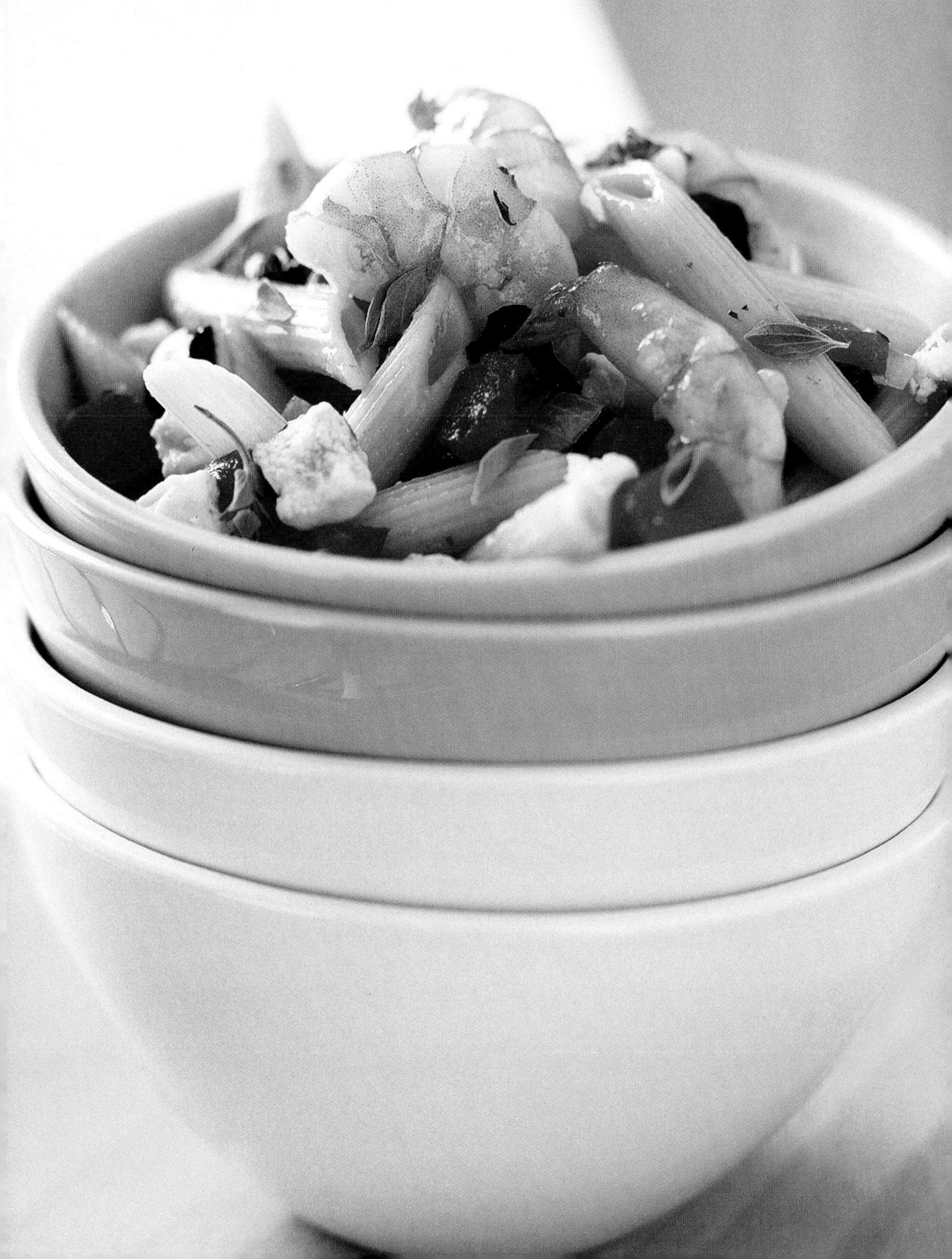

East-Meets-West Shrimp Frittata

Silvia Hendricks, Tiki Island, TX

"My family adores Chinese food," Sylvia writes, "but we're all concerned with our health and weight." This tasty low-fat, egg-foo-yong-like frittata is one way Sylvia has satisfied the family's needs. A variety of meats such as chicken, turkey, or ham can be used instead of the shrimp to make this tasty dish.

2 teaspoons canola oil

1 red bell pepper, seeded and diced

6 scallions, finely chopped

1 celery stalk, diced

1 teaspoon minced peeled fresh ginger

1 garlic clove, minced

1 cup bean sprouts

1 (4-ounce) can shrimp, rinsed and drained

¼ cup sliced water chestnuts, coarsely chopped

2 cups fat-free egg substitute

1 tablespoon oyster sauce

½ teaspoon Asian (dark) sesame oil

MAKES 4 SERVINGS

1. Preheat the broiler.

2. Heat the canola oil in a large ovenproof nonstick skillet over medium-high heat. Add the bell pepper, scallions, and celery. Cook, stirring frequently, until the vegetables are tender and golden, about 8 minutes. Add the ginger and garlic; cook, stirring constantly, until fragrant, about 1 minute. Stir in the bean sprouts, shrimp, and water chestnuts. Cook, stirring occasionally, to blend the flavors, about 3 minutes.

3. Add the egg substitute, oyster sauce, and sesame oil; cook until almost set, lifting the edges frequently with a spatula to let the uncooked egg flow underneath, about 5 minutes.

4. Transfer the skillet to the broiler and broil, 4 inches from the heat, until the top is set and the frittata is cooked through, about 2 minutes. Invert the frittata onto a plate and cut into 4 wedges.

PER SERVING (¼ frittata): 146 Cal, 4 g Fat, 0 g Sat Fat, 0 g Trans Fat, 37 mg Chol, 319 mg Sod, 10 g Carb, 3 g Fib, 19 g Prot, 79 mg Calc. *POINTS* value: 3.

MAIN DISHES

Zucchini and Veggie Burger Pasta

Julie Brandt, Indian Rocks Beach, FL

This meatless version of macaroni and beef is flavorful, satisfying, and ready in under 30 minutes! Julie uses frozen veggie crumbles—a textured vegetable protein, which looks like cooked ground beef, but is made from soybeans. You can find veggie crumbles in the freezer section of many supermarkets and in most health food stores.

1 cup elbow macaroni

2 teaspoons canola oil

1 onion, finely chopped

1 zucchini, diced

1 (12-ounce) package frozen
    veggie crumbles

2 cups prepared
    marinara sauce

MAKES 4 SERVINGS

1. Prepare macaroni according to package directions; drain.

2. Heat the oil in a large nonstick skillet over medium-high heat. Add the onion and cook, stirring occasionally, until softened, about 8 minutes. Add the zucchini and cook until crisp-tender, about 6 minutes. Add the veggie crumbles and marinara sauce; bring to a boil. Reduce the heat and simmer, uncovered, until the flavors are developed, about 10 minutes. Stir in the macaroni and heat through.

PER SERVING (1½ cups): 428 Cal, 8 g Fat, 1 g Sat Fat, 0 g Trans Fat, 0 mg Chol, 531 mg Sod, 51 g Carb, 18 g Fib, 54 g Prot, 302 mg Calc. *POINTS* value: **8.**

MAIN DISHES

Fiesta Stuffed Peppers

Karen Keilson, Granite Bay, CA

"I am totally thrilled with the weight loss I have experienced with your program, and I have changed my eating habits for the better," writes Karen, who reached her goal of losing 12 pounds. She developed this terrific recipe to help with her personal program.

2 teaspoons canola oil

1 onion, finely chopped

1 cup sliced fresh white mushrooms

2 garlic cloves, minced

1 (14½-ounce) can diced tomatoes

1 cup frozen veggie crumbles

1 cup water

½ cup long-grain white rice

2 tablespoons taco seasoning mix

4 large green bell peppers, split in half lengthwise and seeded

MAKES 4 SERVINGS

1. Preheat the oven to 350°F. Spray a 9 x 13-inch baking dish with nonstick spray.

2. Heat the oil in a large nonstick skillet over medium-high heat. Add the onion, mushrooms, and garlic. Cook, stirring occasionally, until softened and lightly browned, about 8 minutes.

3. Add the tomatoes, veggie crumbles, water, rice, and seasoning mix; bring to a boil. Reduce the heat and simmer, covered, until almost all of the liquid is absorbed and the rice is tender, about 15 minutes.

4. Spoon ½ cup of the mixture into each bell pepper half and arrange them in the baking dish. Cover tightly with foil and bake until the bell peppers are softened and the filling is heated through, about 30 minutes.

PER SERVING (2 stuffed pepper halves): 280 Cal, 4 g Fat, 0 g Sat Fat, 0 g Trans Fat, 0 mg Chol, 553 mg Sod, 50 g Carb, 10 g Fib, 18 g Prot, 118 mg Calc. *POINTS* value: *5.*

tip For an attractive presentation, use a combination of brightly colored bell peppers— yellow, orange, green, and red.

Veggie Taco Wraps

Yvonne Grimes, North Bend, WA

Yvonne has lost 91 pounds and reached her goal weight! She credits this great accomplishment to "a supportive husband, an incredible Weight Watchers leader, and an enthusiastic group of members." When asked to share something about her weight-loss journey, she remarks, "It really does help to know that there are other people out there who share your struggles and frustrations, as well as your triumphs and accomplishments."

2 teaspoons canola oil

1 onion, chopped

1 red bell pepper, seeded and diced

1 cup thinly sliced fresh white mushrooms

1 garlic clove, minced

1 tablespoon chili powder

1 teaspoon ground cumin

¼ teaspoon salt

2 cups frozen veggie crumbles

1 cup canned black beans, rinsed and drained

1 cup jarred salsa

¼ cup water

¼ cup chopped fresh cilantro

8 large green leaf or Bibb lettuce leaves

2 tomatoes, diced (about 1 cup)

½ cup fat-free sour cream

½ cup shredded reduced-fat cheddar cheese

MAKES 4 SERVINGS

1. Heat the oil in a large nonstick skillet over medium-high heat. Add the onion, bell pepper, mushrooms, and garlic. Cook, stirring occasionally, until browned, about 8 minutes. Stir in the chili powder, cumin, and salt; cook until fragrant, about 1 minute.

2. Add the veggie crumbles, beans, salsa, and water; bring to a boil. Reduce the heat and simmer, uncovered, until the flavors are blended and the mixture thickens slightly, about 5 minutes. Remove from the heat and stir in the cilantro.

3. Spoon about ½ cup of the mixture onto each lettuce leaf. Top each with 2 tablespoons of the tomatoes and 1 tablespoon each of the sour cream and cheese. Roll up, then cut diagonally in half.

PER SERVING (2 rolls): 348 Cal, 9 g Fat, 3 g Sat Fat, 0 g Trans Fat, 13 mg Chol, 608 mg Sod, 41 g Carb, 15 g Fib, 38 g Prot, 352 mg Calc. *POINTS* value: **7.**

MAIN DISHES

MEATLESS CHEESE
STEAK PITAS

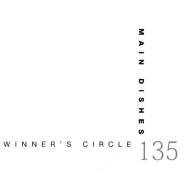

Meatless Cheese Steak Pitas

Penn Collins, Atlanta, GA

Penn has lost "42 pounds and counting" on the program so far! He loves Philly cheese steaks and writes, "I was craving a big, gooey sandwich without exceeding my *POINTS* Target for the day." He solved his craving by creating this easy, vegetarian version. It goes nicely with a cucumber and red onion salad dressed with balsamic vinaigrette.

1 teaspoon canola oil

1 onion, thinly sliced

1 green bell pepper, seeded and thinly sliced

1 cup thinly sliced fresh white mushrooms

½ teaspoon salt

2 cups frozen veggie crumbles

2 (6½-inch) whole-wheat pita breads, halved crosswise

½ cup shredded reduced-fat cheddar cheese

MAKES 4 SERVINGS

1. Heat the oil in a large nonstick skillet over medium-high heat. Add the onion, bell pepper, mushrooms, and salt. Cook, stirring frequently, until softened, about 8 minutes. Stir in the veggie crumbles and heat through.

2. Spoon ¾ cup of the mixture into each pita half; top each with 2 tablespoons of the cheese. Serve at once.

PER SERVING (1 pita half): 290 Cal, 7 g Fat, 2 g Sat Fat, 0 g Trans Fat, 10 mg Chol, 470 mg Sod, 35 g Carb, 11 g Fib, 34 g Prot, 250 mg Calc. **POINTS** value: **6.**

tip For variety, divide the filling among four warmed fat-free flour tortillas, sprinkle with the cheese, roll up, and cut diagonally in half.

Vegetarian Chili

Kathy Kemnetz, Arlington Heights, IL

Our thanks go to Kathy's understanding family. She writes, "They ate a lot of chili before I hit on the right combination." Now that she has it, she plans to make this a favorite anytime they feel like a good vegetarian meal. You can serve it with fresh baked corn bread—a 2-inch square increases the *POINTS* value by 3.

2 teaspoons olive oil

1 onion, finely chopped

1 green bell pepper, seeded and diced

2 garlic cloves, minced

3 tablespoons chili powder

1 teaspoon ground cumin

1 teaspoon dried oregano

½ teaspoon salt

1 (15½-ounce) can black beans, rinsed and drained

1 (15½-ounce) can chickpeas (garbanzo beans), rinsed and drained

1 (14½-ounce) can diced tomatoes

2 cups low-sodium chicken broth

1 zucchini, diced

1 (10-ounce) package frozen chopped spinach, thawed and squeezed dry

MAKES 6 SERVINGS

1. Heat the oil in a large nonstick saucepan over medium-high heat. Add the onion, bell pepper, and garlic. Cook, stirring frequently, until softened, about 8 minutes. Stir in the chili powder, cumin, oregano, and salt; cook until fragrant, about 1 minute.

2. Add the beans, chickpeas, tomatoes, broth, and zucchini; bring to a boil. Reduce the heat and simmer, covered, until the flavors are blended and the chili thickens slightly, about 20 minutes. Stir in the spinach and heat through.

PER SERVING (2 cups): 165 Cal, 4 g Fat, 1 g Sat Fat, 0 g Trans Fat, 1 mg Chol, 565 mg Sod, 25 g Carb, 9 g Fib, 9 g Prot, 129 mg Calc. *POINTS* value: 3.

Soft Tacos with Goat Cheese and Mango Salsa

Jon McDunn, Poway, CA

Jon and his wife remember eating a high-fat version of these tacos at a restaurant on their wedding night. In trying to make a low-*POINTS* value version, they decided to add beans for fiber and use a flavorful cheese. "It still reminds us of the original, but now it's healthy," says Jon.

1 ripe mango, peeled and cubed

1 cup canned black beans, rinsed and drained

½ red bell pepper, seeded and diced

¼ cup chopped fresh cilantro

3 scallions, finely chopped

1 tablespoon fresh lime juice

1 tablespoon honey

¼ teaspoon salt

4 (8-inch) fat-free flour tortillas, warmed

¼ cup crumbled reduced-fat goat cheese

MAKES 4 SERVINGS

1. Combine the mango, beans, bell pepper, cilantro, scallions, lime juice, honey, and salt in a large bowl.

2. Spoon a generous ½ cup of the mango mixture onto each warmed tortilla. Sprinkle each with 1 tablespoon of the goat cheese. Roll up the tortillas, then cut each diagonally in half.

PER SERVING (1 taco): 240 Cal, 5 g Fat, 2 g Sat Fat, 0 g Trans Fat, 3 mg Chol, 367 mg Sod, 40 g Carb, 7 g Fib, 10 g Prot, 352 mg Calc. *POINTS* value: 4.

tip To warm the tortillas, place on a microwavable plate. Cover with a damp paper towel and microwave on High for about a minute.

Veggie Enchiladas

Lori Monroe, Clarksburg, CA

Lori's husband, Jim, inspired this tasty creation. "He said, rather desperately, 'Honey, if we become vegetarians, I'll never get your enchiladas again!' I promised him that I would make enchiladas that were so good, he wouldn't miss the meat," says Lori. We didn't either.

2 teaspoons canola oil

2 (4-ounce) Portobello mushrooms, coarsely chopped

1 cup white mushrooms, coarsely chopped

1 zucchini, diced

4 scallions, thinly sliced

2 garlic cloves, minced

1 teaspoon adobo seasoning

1 (19-ounce) can enchilada sauce

6 (8-inch) fat-free flour tortillas

6 tablespoons fat-free sour cream

½ cup shredded reduced-fat cheddar cheese

¼ cup sliced ripe olives

MAKES 6 SERVINGS

1. Preheat the oven to 375°F. Spray a 9 x 13-inch baking dish with nonstick spray.

2. Heat the oil in a large nonstick skillet over medium-high heat. Add the Portobello and white mushrooms, the zucchini, scallions, garlic, and seasoning. Cook, stirring occasionally, until any liquid has evaporated and the vegetables are tender, about 6 minutes. Stir in ¼ cup of the enchilada sauce; heat through.

3. Meanwhile, wrap the tortillas in foil and place in the oven to warm, about 10 minutes.

4. Top each tortilla with one-sixth of the mushroom mixture, then with 1 tablespoon of the sour cream. Roll up and place, seam-side down, in the baking dish. Spoon the remaining enchilada sauce over the top. Sprinkle with the cheese and olives. Cover with foil and bake 15 minutes. Uncover and bake until the edges of the enchiladas just begin to brown, and the cheese is melted, about 10 minutes longer. Let stand 5 minutes before serving.

PER SERVING (1 enchilada): 211 Cal, 7 g Fat, 2 g Sat Fat, 0 g Trans Fat, 8 mg Chol, 800 mg Sod, 31 g Carb, 4 g Fib, 7 g Prot, 111 mg Calc. *POINTS* value: **4.**

Roasted Spaghetti Squash with Garlic, Broccoli, and Tomatoes

Sally A. McKinnon, North Tonawanda, NY

This pale yellow, oval-shaped winter squash gets its name from its flesh, which—after baking and scraping pasta-like strands from it—looks like spaghetti. It's great here with vegetables, but it can also be served with your favorite tomato sauce.

1 (5-pound) spaghetti squash,
halved lengthwise
and seeded

2 cups broccoli florets

1 tablespoon extra-virgin
olive oil

3 garlic cloves, minced

2 large tomatoes,
coarsely chopped

½ teaspoon salt

½ teaspoon freshly
ground pepper

3 tablespoons grated
Parmesan cheese

MAKES 4 SERVINGS

1. Preheat the oven to 400°F. Spray a medium baking dish with nonstick spray. Pierce the squash in several places with the tip of a sharp knife and place in the baking dish. Cover with foil and bake until the squash is fork-tender, about 1 hour. Let stand 5 minutes. With a fork, drag through the flesh, pulling the strands apart; transfer to a large bowl and set aside.

2. Bring a medium pot of water to a boil. Add the broccoli and cook until crisp-tender, 3–4 minutes, drain.

3. Heat the oil in a large nonstick skillet over medium heat. Add the garlic and cook, stirring constantly, until fragrant, about 1 minute. Add the tomatoes, salt, and pepper; bring to a boil. Reduce the heat and simmer, uncovered, until the tomatoes are softened, 3–4 minutes. Stir in the squash and broccoli. Cook, tossing frequently, until heated through, about 2 minutes. Serve sprinkled with the cheese.

PER SERVING (1½ cups): 210 Cal, 6 g Fat, 2 g Sat Fat, 0 g Trans Fat, 3 mg Chol, 466 mg Sod, 38 g Carb, 9 g Fib, 7 g Prot, 180 mg Calc. *POINTS* value: 4.

Roasted Vegetable Omelette

Jane Ronis, Port Washington, NY

Jane feels that her Weight Watchers group has the most inspirational leader, who "keeps us laughing and shows us that no matter what life might deal you, you can succeed." Jane has certainly found success with this egg white omelette, chock-full of sweet and delicious roasted veggies.

1 zucchini, diced

1 yellow squash, diced

1 green bell pepper, seeded and diced

1 all-purpose potato, diced

1 tomato, diced

1 onion, diced

1 tablespoon chopped fresh rosemary

½ teaspoon salt

½ teaspoon freshly ground pepper

6 egg whites, lightly beaten

¼ cup light cream cheese with herbs, cubed

MAKES 4 SERVINGS

1. Arrange one rack on the bottom rung of the oven. Preheat the oven to 450°F.

2. Combine the zucchini, yellow squash, bell pepper, potato, tomato, onion, rosemary, salt, and pepper in a large bowl; lightly spray with olive-oil nonstick spray. Spread the vegetables in a large nonstick baking sheet. Roast, on the bottom rack of the oven, stirring occasionally, until the vegetables are tender and browned, about 25 minutes.

3. Spray a large nonstick skillet with nonstick spray and set over medium heat. Add the egg whites and cook until just set, 3–4 minutes, lifting the edges frequently with a spatula to let the uncooked egg flow underneath. Spoon the vegetable mixture over the eggs, then sprinkle the cheese. Cover the skillet and cook until the cheese melts, 2–3 minutes. Fold the omelette in half and slide out onto a plate.

PER SERVING (¼ of omelette): 145 Cal, 3 g Fat, 2 g Sat Fat, 0 g Trans Fat, 8 mg Chol, 475 mg Sod, 21 g Carb, 4 g Fib, 10 g Prot, 59 mg Calc. *POINTS* value: *2.*

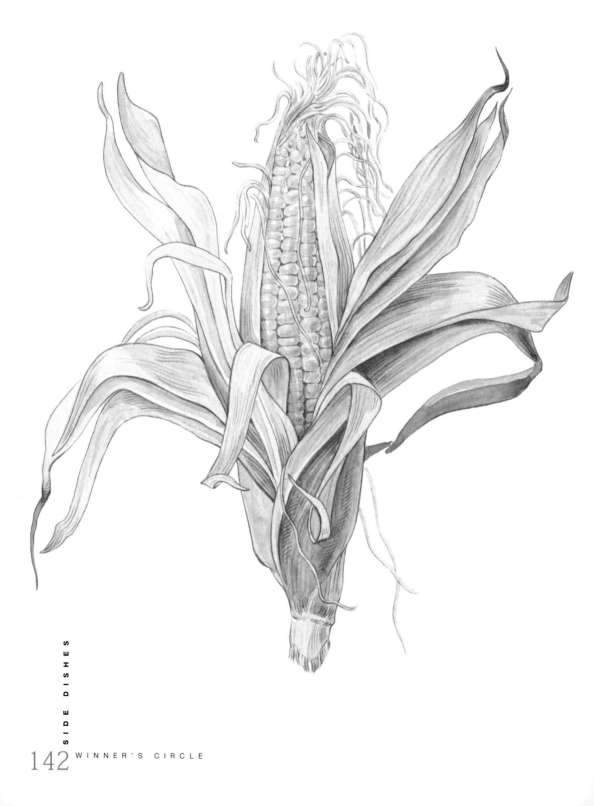

CHAPTER 4

Side Dishes

FROM GREEN BEANS TO CORN TO QUINOA

Southwestern Squash

Michael R. Zelenak, Fridley, MN

"Fabulous and flavorful," is how Michael describes his prize-winning recipe. And we couldn't agree with him more! The combination of prepared hummus, honey, and cumin gives this tasty dish its unique flavor. Roasted red pepper hummus can be found in the refrigerated section of most supermarkets. If it's not available, use regular hummus instead and add 2 teaspoons of diced pimientos.

1 acorn squash (about 1¾ pounds)

2 tablespoons prepared roasted red pepper hummus

1 tablespoon honey

1 teaspoon ground cumin

½ teaspoon salt

¼ teaspoon crushed red pepper

1 tablespoon shredded Parmesan cheese

MAKES 4 SERVINGS

1. Preheat the oven to 400°F. Line a baking sheet with foil; spray the foil with nonstick spray. Spray a 7 x 11-inch baking dish with nonstick spray; set aside. Cut the squash in half, discard the seeds, and place the squash, cut-side down, on the baking sheet. Bake until the squash is tender, 35–45 minutes. Leave the oven on.

2. Remove the squash from the oven and set aside until cool enough to handle. Scoop out the flesh and place in a medium bowl. Discard the skin.

3. Add the hummus, honey, cumin, salt, and crushed red pepper to the squash in the bowl; mix well. Spread the mixture into the baking dish. Sprinkle with the cheese. Bake until the squash is heated through and the cheese is lightly browned, about 15 minutes.

PER SERVING (½ cup): 114 Cal, 2 g Fat, 0 g Sat Fat, 0 g Trans Fat, 1 mg Chol, 350 mg Sod, 26 g Carb, 7 g Fib, 3 g Prot, 85 mg Calc. **POINTS** value: 2.

SIDE DISHES

Home-Style Potato Wedges

Christine Charters, Ontario, Canada

Christine likes to create tasty, light dishes that are reminiscent of her old, high-fat favorites. "These potato wedges are an excellent substitute for French fries," she says. "They are crisp and flavorful, yet low in *POINTS* value. When I have a craving for fries, I make these and am completely satisfied!"

2 egg whites

2 tablespoons water

½ cup cornflake crumbs

3 tablespoons all-purpose flour

3 tablespoons grated
Parmesan cheese

1 teaspoon dried oregano

½ teaspoon salt

½ teaspoon freshly
ground pepper

3 baking potatoes, scrubbed
and cut into ¼-inch wedges

MAKES 4 SERVINGS

1. Preheat the oven to 400°F. Spray a large nonstick baking sheet with nonstick spray.

2. Lightly beat the egg whites and water in a shallow bowl. Mix the cornflake crumbs, flour, cheese, oregano, salt, and pepper on a sheet of wax paper. Dip the potatoes into the egg whites, then into the crumb mixture, and arrange in one layer on the baking sheet. Lightly spray the potatoes with nonstick spray. Bake 20 minutes. Turn the potatoes and lightly spray again with nonstick spray. Bake until the potatoes are tender and crisp, about 20 minutes longer.

PER SERVING (¾ cup): 238 Cal, 1 g Fat, 1 g Sat Fat, 0 g Trans Fat, 3 mg Chol, 484 mg Sod, 48 g Carb, 4 g Fib, 9 g Prot, 85 mg Calc. *POINTS* value: **4.**

HOME-STYLE POTATO WEDGES

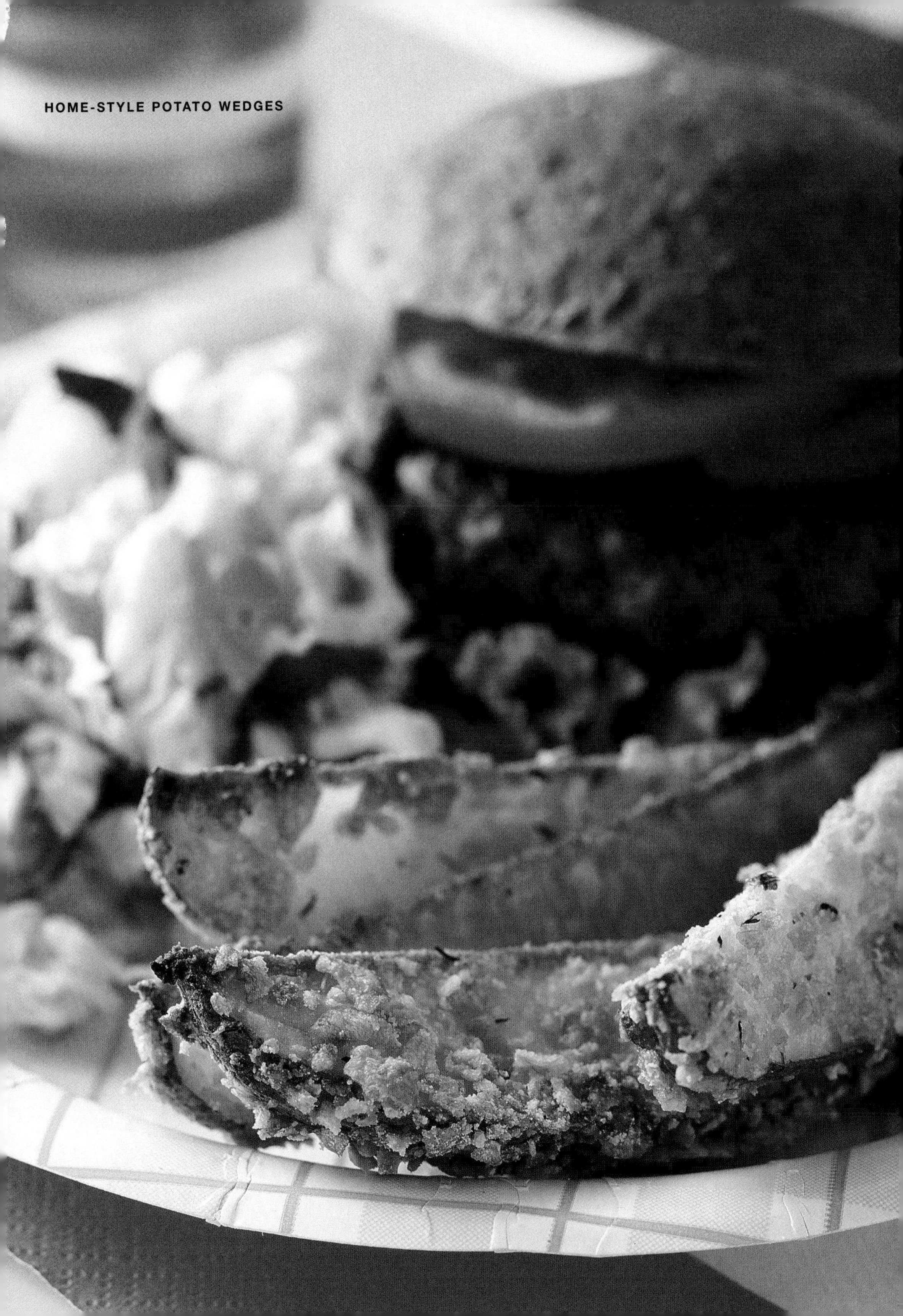

Chili-Topped Potatoes

Dawn Vroom, Lebanon Junction, KY

These flavorful potatoes make a hearty side dish to serve with simple grilled or baked fish. As an option, cut each potato in fourths (so the recipe serves eight) and team it with a more substantial entrée. With a crisp green salad to round out the meal, this Mexican delight could also be a perfect lunch or a light dinner.

2 baking potatoes (about 1¼ pounds), scrubbed

1 teaspoon canola oil

1 onion, chopped

1 tablespoon chili powder

1 (14½-ounce) can Mexican-style stewed tomatoes, drained

½ cup frozen whole-kernel corn, thawed

½ cup canned pinto beans, rinsed and drained

¼ cup shredded reduced-fat cheddar cheese

¼ cup chopped fresh cilantro

MAKES 4 SERVINGS

1. Preheat the oven to 425°F. Prick the potatoes in several places with a fork, place on the middle oven rack, and bake until fork-tender, 45–55 minutes.

2. Heat the oil in a large nonstick skillet over medium heat. Add the onion and cook, stirring occasionally, until tender, about 8 minutes. Add the chili powder and cook 1 minute. Stir in the tomatoes, corn, and beans; bring to a boil. Reduce the heat and simmer, uncovered, until the flavors are blended and the chili thickens slightly, 10–12 minutes.

3. Split the potatoes lengthwise in half to make 4 halves. Fluff the pulp with a fork. Spoon one-fourth of the chili on top of each half. Sprinkle with the cheese and cilantro.

PER SERVING (1 potato half with generous ⅓ cup chili and 1 tablespoon cheese): 257 Cal, 3 g Fat, 1 g Sat Fat, 0 g Trans Fat, 5 mg Chol, 480 mg Sod, 50 g Carb, 8 g Fib, 9 g Prot, 112 mg Calc. *POINTS* value: 5.

Potato-Garlic Crisps

Laurel A. Wendell, Mt. Kisco, NY

Laurel, with the help of her "so supportive" leader, has lost 24 pounds and is a Lifetime member. She makes these crispy potatoes, on request, for her daughter and friends. These tasty bites also make great appetizers when entertaining.

2 large Yukon Gold potatoes,
  (about 1 pound) cut into
  ⅛-inch-thick slices
¾ teaspoon garlic salt
½ teaspoon dried oregano
½ teaspoon freshly
  ground pepper

MAKES 4 SERVINGS

1. Preheat the oven to 425°F. Spray a large baking sheet with nonstick spray.

2. Combine the potatoes, garlic salt, oregano, and pepper in a large bowl. Arrange the potatoes in one layer on the baking sheet. Lightly spray with nonstick spray. Bake until the potatoes are tender and crisp, about 40 minutes.

PER SERVING (¾ cup): 94 Cal, 1 g Fat, 0 g Sat Fat, 0 g Trans Fat, 0 mg Chol, 344 mg Sod, 21 g Carb, 2 g Fib, 2 g Prot, 20 mg Calc. **POINTS** value: *2*.

tip The success of this recipe depends, in part, on having very thinly sliced potatoes. The perfect tool for such a cutting task is a mandoline—a hand-operated slicing machine. Professional-quality stainless steel mandolines are effective, but pricey. Less expensive, plastic models with stainless steel blades work just as well.

Creamy Whipped Potatoes

Tiffany Leger-Rodriguez, Placentia, CA

"I used to think that if I just exercised enough, I could eat however much I wanted. My body proved me wrong! Weight Watchers helped to show me that portion control and moderate exercise equal weight-loss success," says Tiffany, who lost 18 pounds and is now a Lifetime member. The scallions add color and texture to this slimmed down, yet creamy, mash.

2 baking potatoes (about 1½ pounds), peeled and cubed
¼ cup low-sodium chicken broth
¼ cup reduced-fat sour cream
¼ cup fat-free cream cheese, at room temperature
½ teaspoon salt
¼ teaspoon freshly ground pepper
¼ cup chopped scallions

MAKES 4 SERVINGS

1. Place the potatoes and enough water to cover in a large saucepan; bring to a boil. Reduce the heat and simmer, covered, until the potatoes are tender, about 20 minutes. Drain; transfer to a large bowl.

2. Add the broth, sour cream, cream cheese, salt, and pepper. With an electric mixer on medium speed, beat the potatoes until smooth and creamy. Stir in the scallions.

PER SERVING (generous ½ cup): 168 Cal, 2 g Fat, 1 g Sat Fat, 0 g Trans Fat, 9 mg Chol, 393 mg Sod, 32 g Carb, 3 g Fib, 6 g Prot, 65 mg Calc. *POINTS* value: **3**.

Creamed Potatoes Florentine

Jackie Negaard, Bettendorf, IA

Jackie has lost 22 pounds and is a Weight Watchers Lifetime member. She faithfully goes to meetings because the "support of the group makes the difference between gaining one pound instead of five, or of eating one piece of cake instead of the whole thing." Jackie adjusted a recipe her mom used to make—which called for lots of cream, butter, and a pound or more of crispy bacon pieces—and created this delicious dish.

1 pound all-purpose potatoes, peeled and cubed

1 teaspoon olive oil

1 (9-ounce) bag baby spinach leaves

1 garlic clove, minced

⅓ cup fat-free half-and-half

½ teaspoon salt

⅛ teaspoon nutmeg

MAKES 4 SERVINGS

1. Place the potatoes and enough water to cover in a large saucepan; bring to a boil. Reduce the heat and simmer, covered, until the potatoes are tender, about 20 minutes. Drain; return to the saucepan. Coarsely mash the potatoes with a fork; keep warm.

2. Heat the oil in a medium nonstick skillet over medium-high heat. Add the spinach and garlic; cook, stirring occasionally, until the spinach wilts, about 3 minutes.

3. Add the spinach mixture to the potatoes in the saucepan; Stir in the half-and-half, salt, and nutmeg; heat through.

PER SERVING (generous ½ cup): 123 Cal, 2 g Fat, 0 g Sat Fat, 0 g Trans Fat, 0 mg Chol, 362 mg Sod, 24 g Carb, 4 g Fib, 4 g Prot, 96 mg Calc.
POINTS value: 2.

tip If it's more convenient, you can use a 10-ounce package of frozen chopped spinach in place of the baby spinach. Just make sure it is thawed and squeezed dry before adding to the potato mixture.

Spicy Sweet Potato Fries

Anika Ansetta, Berkeley Heights, NJ

Anika, who is always trying to come up with low-fat, healthy recipes, and is forever on the lookout for ways to incorporate more veggies into her diet, created these wonderful spicy fries. "I even taught my boyfriend how to make them, since he loves them so much," writes Anika, who eats them as a side dish or snack. You might like to try them with grilled turkey burgers and a cool mango salsa.

2 large sweet potatoes (about 1¾ pounds), peeled and cut into ¼-inch-thick wedges
1 tablespoon chili powder
1 tablespoon Cajun seasoning
2 teaspoons olive oil

MAKES 4 SERVINGS

1. Preheat the oven to 400°F. Spray a large baking sheet with nonstick spray.

2. Combine the potatoes, chili powder, Cajun seasoning, and oil in a large bowl. Spread the potatoes in one layer on the baking sheet. Bake until tender and golden, 30–40 minutes.

PER SERVING (generous ½ cup): 152 Cal, 3 g Fat, 0 g Sat Fat, 0 g Trans Fat, 0 mg Chol, 89 mg Sod, 31 g Carb, 4 g Fib, 2 g Prot, 39 mg Calc. **POINTS** value: 2.

SIDE DISHES

Blissful Veggie Rice

Jeanette Hernandez, Miramar, FL

Jeanette has lost 16½ pounds on the Program. She believes in healthy eating and tries to include plenty of vegetables in her and her family's diet. "I find the children enjoy eating their veggies when I incorporate them into great tasting recipes like this," she writes. This homey side deliciously complements any broiled, grilled, or baked meats, poultry, or fish. Leftovers can easily transform into a salad: Simply chill the rice mixture, then toss with sliced fresh mushrooms, chopped tomatoes, diced cucumber, and a sprinkle of your favorite fat-free dressing.

2 teaspoons olive oil

1 onion, finely chopped

1 carrot, diced

1 zucchini, diced

½ teaspoon salt

¼ teaspoon freshly
  ground pepper

1 cup instant brown rice

1 cup low-sodium
  chicken broth

2 tablespoons chopped parsley

MAKES 4 SERVINGS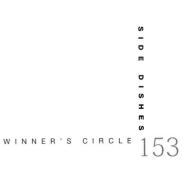

1. Heat the oil in a large nonstick skillet over medium-high heat. Add the onion and carrot. Cook, stirring frequently, until tender, about 6 minutes. Stir in the zucchini, salt, and pepper; cook until just tender, about 3 minutes.

2. Add the rice, broth, and parsley; bring to a boil. Remove from the heat. Let stand, covered, until the liquid is absorbed, about 5 minutes.

PER SERVING (generous ½ cup): 144 Cal, 4 g Fat, 1 g Sat Fat, 0 g Trans Fat, 1 mg Chol, 336 mg Sod, 25 g Carb, 3 g Fib, 4 g Prot, 28 mg Calc.
POINTS value: **3.**

RICE-STUFFED TOMATOES

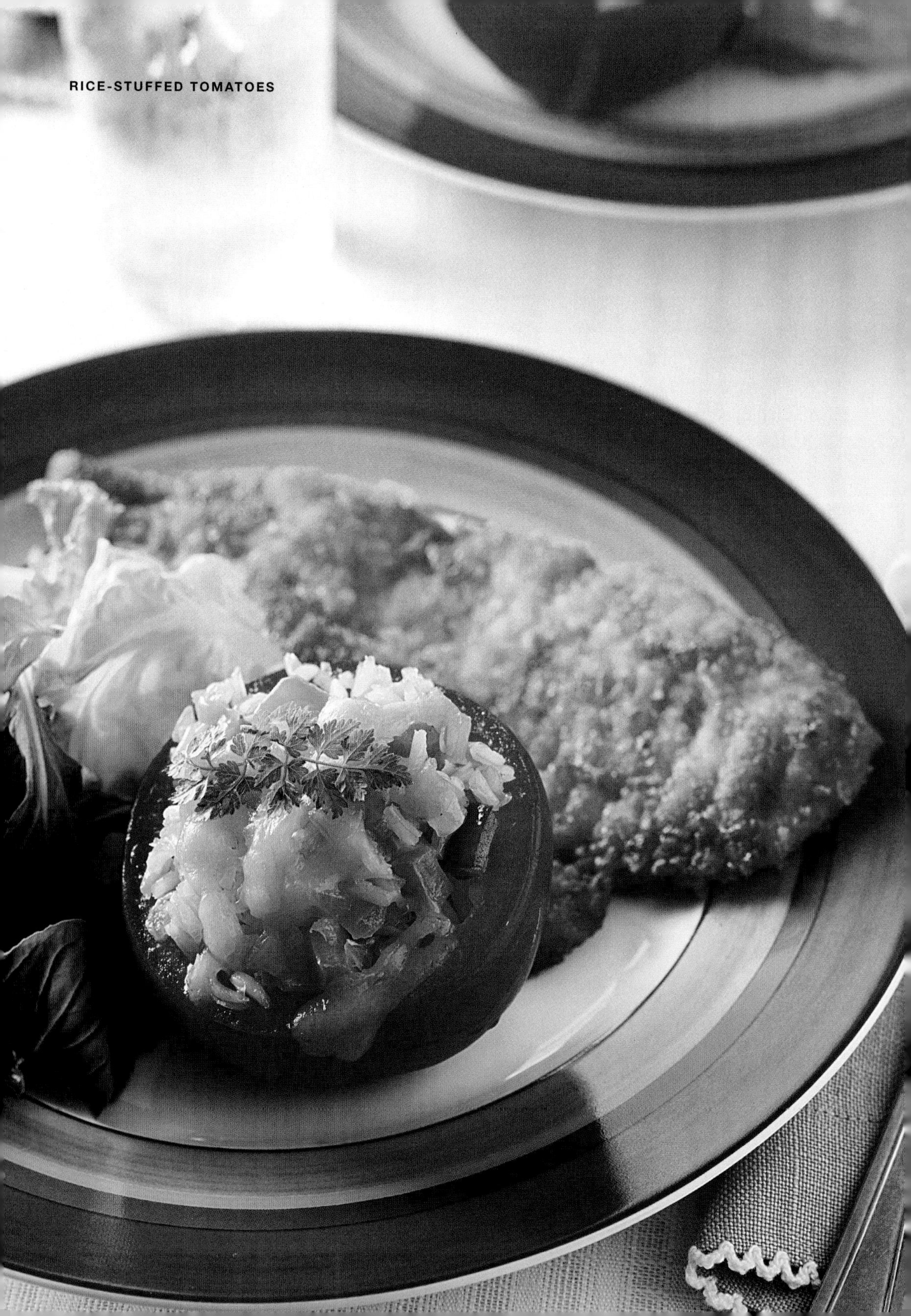

Rice-Stuffed Tomatoes

Misty Jones, Latham, NY

Misty, who has lost 17 pounds on the program so far, says, "I actually enjoy my food more since joining Weight Watchers. I choose from a greater selection of foods and seem to eat more." This tasty side also works nicely as a light lunch.

2	teaspoons olive oil
1	onion, finely chopped
1	carrot, finely chopped
½	green bell pepper, seeded and chopped
2	cups cooked brown rice
1½	teaspoon salt
2	large tomatoes
¼	cup shredded reduced-fat cheddar cheese

MAKES 4 SERVINGS

1. Heat the oil in a large nonstick skillet over medium-high heat. Add the onion, carrot, and bell pepper. Cook, stirring frequently, until softened, about 8 minutes. Stir in the rice and salt; remove from the heat.

2. Preheat the oven to 400°F. Spray a 7 x 11-inch baking dish with nonstick spray.

3. Cut each tomato crosswise in half. Remove a small slice from the bottom of each tomato half to prevent from rolling. With a spoon, scoop out the seeds and flesh (save for soups, stews, etc.). Fill each tomato half with ½ cup of the rice mixture. Place the tomatoes in the baking dish. Sprinkle each half with 1 tablespoon of the cheese. Bake until filling is hot and the cheese melts, about 15 minutes.

PER SERVING (1 stuffed tomato half): 195 Cal, 5 g Fat, 2 g Sat Fat, 0 g Trans Fat, 5 mg Chol, 315 mg Sod, 33 g Carb, 4 g Fib, 6 g Prot, 79 mg Calc.
POINTS value: **4.**

SIDE DISHES

Scallion Corn Pudding

Beverly A. Parker Virginia Beach, VA

"My husband would often ask me to make corn pudding—a favorite dish in Virginia. Every recipe I found called for lots of butter, eggs, and cream. I was determined to make a healthier version," writes Beverly. Now she and her husband enjoy this favorite without the fat and calories. Serve with tomato salsa, if you like.

2 teaspoons olive oil

6 scallions, finely chopped

1 (10-ounce) package frozen whole-kernel corn, thawed

½ cup low-fat (1%) milk

½ cup fat-free egg substitute

¼ cup shredded reduced-fat cheddar cheese

1 tablespoon all-purpose flour

1 teaspoon sugar

MAKES 4 SERVINGS

1. Preheat the oven to 375°F. Spray an 8-inch square baking dish with nonstick spray.

2. Heat the oil in a small nonstick skillet over medium-high heat. Add the scallions and cook, stirring, until softened, about 3 minutes. Transfer to a large bowl. Add the corn, milk, egg substitute, cheese, flour, and sugar. Scrape the mixture into the baking dish. Bake until slightly puffed and cooked through, 35–40 minutes.

PER SERVING (¼ of pudding): 147 Cal, 5 g Fat, 2 g Sat Fat, 0 g Trans Fat, 6 mg Chol, 83 mg Sod, 21 g Carb, 2 g Fib, 8 g Prot, 114 mg Calc. *POINTS* value: **3.**

SIDE DISHES

Quinoa with Peppers, Tomatoes, and Feta

Pamela Dickson, Germantown, MD

Lifetime member Pamela, who has lost 16 pounds, says, "Weight Watchers has changed my life. I have taught myself to cook differently and to exercise regularly. I'm really happy!" Quinoa, a grain native to South America, is gaining popularity in American markets. Pamela has put her new healthy habits to good use in this delicious side dish.

2 cups water

1 cup quinoa, rinsed
    and drained

1 teaspoon olive oil

1 onion, finely chopped

1 green bell pepper, seeded
    and diced

2 plum tomatoes, chopped

½ teaspoon salt

¼ teaspoon freshly
    ground pepper

2 tablespoons crumbled
    reduced-fat feta cheese

2 tablespoons chopped parsley

MAKES 4 SERVINGS

1. Bring the water to a boil in a saucepan; stir in the quinoa. Reduce the heat and simmer, covered, until tender and most of the water evaporates, about 10 minutes; drain.

2. Heat the oil in a large nonstick skillet over medium-high heat. Add the onion and bell pepper and cook, stirring frequently, until tender, about 6 minutes. Stir in the tomatoes, salt, and pepper and cook until soft, about 5 minutes. Stir in the quinoa; heat through. Remove from the heat. Gently fold in the feta cheese and parsley.

PER SERVING (1 cup): 212 Cal, 5 g Fat, 1 g Sat Fat, 0 g Trans Fat, 3 mg Chol, 398 mg Sod, 37 g Carb, 4 g Fib, 8 g Prot, 54 mg Calc. **POINTS** value: **4.**

tip Be sure to rinse quinoa grains thoroughly under cold running water for about 1 minute before cooking to remove the bitter outer coating.

SIDE DISHES

Cottage Cheese Kugel

Cheri Silver, Buffalo Grove, IL

Cheri likes to alter family-favorite recipes to fit the Weight Watchers profile—and this slimmed-down kugel, a sweet or savory baked pudding usually made with noodles or potatoes, is a perfect example. Cheri serves her kugel as a delicious side dish, but it also works as a dessert or brunch dish too. If you like, add ¼ cup golden raisins to the mixture before baking.

8 ounces wide egg noodles

1 cup low-fat (1%) cottage cheese

½ cup low-fat (1%) milk

⅓ cup fat-free egg substitute

¼ cup fat-free sour cream

3 tablespoons sugar

1 teaspoon vanilla extract

½ teaspoon cinnamon

¼ cup cornflake crumbs

MAKES 6 SERVINGS

1. Preheat the oven to 375°F. Spray an 8-inch square baking dish with nonstick spray.

2. Cook the noodles according to package directions. Drain and transfer to a large bowl. Add the cottage cheese, milk, egg substitute, sour cream, sugar, vanilla, and cinnamon.

3. Spoon the noodle mixture evenly into the baking dish. Sprinkle the crumbs on top. Bake, uncovered, until the filling is set and the top is golden, about 35 minutes. Let stand 5 minutes before serving.

PER SERVING (scant 1 cup): 234 Cal, 2 g Fat, 1 g Sat Fat, 0 g Trans Fat, 42 mg Chol, 234 mg Sod, 40 g Carb, 1 g Fib, 13 g Prot, 81 mg Calc.
POINTS value: *5.*

Ginger-Sesame Green Beans

Jiya Sarma, Weehawken, NJ

By using just a few simple ingredients, Jiya has created a tasty, Asian-inspired dish. "This is a fusion-style recipe, which I love because my marriage is fusion too! My husband is Indian and I am American," says Jiya. "We both love this recipe because of its big, bold flavors and it's easy to make," You could substitute broccoli, asparagus, snow peas, or sugar snap peas for the green beans, if you like.

½ pound fresh green beans, trimmed and cut diagonally into 2-inch pieces (about 2 cups)

1 teaspoon canola oil

2 garlic cloves, minced

2 teaspoons minced peeled fresh ginger

2 teaspoons reduced-sodium soy sauce

½ teaspoon Asian (dark) sesame oil

1 teaspoon toasted sesame seeds

MAKES 4 SERVINGS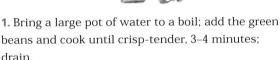

1. Bring a large pot of water to a boil; add the green beans and cook until crisp-tender, 3–4 minutes; drain.

2. Heat the canola oil in a large nonstick saucepan over medium-high heat. Add the garlic and ginger; cook, stirring, until fragrant, about 1 minute. Stir in the green beans, soy sauce, and sesame oil; heat through. Remove from the heat and sprinkle with the sesame seeds.

PER SERVING (½ cup): 44 Cal, 2 g Fat, 0 g Sat Fat, 0 g Trans Fat, 0 mg Chol, 103 mg Sod, 5 g Carb, 2 g Fib, 2 g Prot, 38 mg Calc. *POINTS* value: 1.

tip To toast the sesame seeds, place them in a dry skillet, over medium-low heat. Cook, shaking the pan and stirring constantly, until fragrant, 1 to 2 minutes. Watch them carefully; since they can burn quickly. Transfer the seeds to a plate to cool.

SIDE DISHES

Greek-Style Green Beans

Elaine Sutherland, New York, NY

"I am of Greek descent," writes Elaine "and my grandmother and mother have made this Greek favorite for years for family gatherings and holidays. The green beans are cooked until tender and soft, not crunchy, and everyone loves them." Elaine enjoys eating this with a slice of crusty peasant bread to soak up the juices.

½ pound fresh green beans

2 teaspoons olive oil

1 onion, finely chopped

1 celery stalk, finely chopped

1 garlic clove, minced

1 (14½-ounce) can Italian stewed tomatoes

½ teaspoon dried oregano

¼ teaspoon freshly ground pepper

MAKES 4 SERVINGS

1. Bring a pot of water to a boil; add the green beans and cook until very tender, 8–10 minutes; drain.

2. Heat the oil in a large nonstick skillet over medium-high heat. Add the onion, celery, and garlic; cook, stirring occasionally, until tender, about 8 minutes. Add the tomatoes, oregano, and pepper; bring to a boil. Reduce the heat and simmer, covered, until the tomatoes are soft and the flavors are blended, 10–12 minutes. Stir in the beans and heat through.

PER SERVING (generous ½ cup): 84 Cal, 3 g Fat, 0 g Sat Fat, 0 g Trans Fat, 0 mg Chol, 358 mg Sod, 15 g Carb, 5 g Fib, 3 g Prot, 60 mg Calc. *POINTS* value: *1.*

SIDE DISHES

Glazed Carrots

Michael W. Cervone, Philadelphia, PA

Michael has been a member of Weight Watchers for three decades and loves to collect Weight Watchers cookbooks. Since carrots are one of his "favorite veggies," he serves this sweet side with many of his meals. You might like to try them with grilled pork tenderloin, broiled chicken, or baked fish.

4 medium carrots, thinly sliced diagonally

½ cup water

2 teaspoons butter

1 tablespoon orange juice

1 tablespoon honey

¼ teaspoon cinnamon

⅛ teaspoon nutmeg

⅛ teaspoon salt

MAKES 4 SERVINGS

1. Bring the carrots, water, and butter to a boil in a medium skillet over medium-high heat. Cover and cook until the liquid evaporates and the carrots are crisp-tender, 4–5 minutes.

2. Add the orange juice, honey, cinnamon, nutmeg, and salt. Cook until the carrots are glazed and lightly browned, about 3 minutes.

PER SERVING (½ cup): 62 Cal, 2 g Fat, 1 g Sat Fat, 0 g Trans Fat, 5 mg Chol, 95 mg Sod, 11 g Carb, 2 g Fib, 1 g Prot, 20 mg Calc. *POINTS* value: *1*.

SIDE DISHES

Balsamic-Glazed Roasted Onions

Jan Johns, Boise, ID

Jan first made these delicious sweet roasted onions for a Thanksgiving dinner and liked them so much she now serves them throughout the year. In the winter, she teams them with pork, chicken, or turkey; in summer, with grilled salmon.

2 large onions (about 1½ pounds) cut into 1-inch-thick wedges

3 tablespoons balsamic vinegar

1 tablespoon extra-virgin olive oil

1 garlic clove, minced

¼ teaspoon freshly ground pepper

1 tablespoon grated Parmesan cheese

1 tablespoon chopped fresh thyme

MAKES 4 SERVINGS

1. Preheat the oven to 425°F. Spray a 9 x 13-inch baking dish with nonstick spray. Arrange the onion wedges, overlapping slightly, in the baking dish.

2. Whisk together the vinegar, oil, garlic, and pepper. Drizzle the vinegar mixture over the onions.

3. Bake, uncovered, until the onions are tender and glazed, about 45 minutes. Sprinkle with the cheese and thyme. Serve hot or at room temperature.

PER SERVING (¾ cup): 109 Cal, 4 g Fat, 1 g Sat Fat, 0 g Trans Fat, 1 mg Chol, 31 mg Sod, 17 g Carb, 2 g Fib, 3 g Prot, 57 mg Calc. *POINTS* value: 2.

**BALSAMIC-GLAZED
ROASTED ONIONS**

Crunchy Baked Onion Rings

Marilyn Slater, Ontario, Canada

Recently, Marilyn and her husband have been trying to replace high-fat, fast food with healthier alternatives. "When the craving for fast food hits, I serve these onion rings with turkey or veggie burgers along with a fruit smoothie," she says. The crunchy cornflake coating makes them taste like the real deal.

2 egg whites

2 tablespoons cold water

1½ cups cornflake crumbs

¼ teaspoon salt

1 Spanish onion (about 1 pound), cut into ¼-inch-thick rings

MAKES 4 SERVINGS

1. Arrange one oven rack on the second rung from the bottom. Preheat the oven to 425°F. Spray a large baking sheet with nonstick spray.

2. Whisk together the egg whites and water in a pie plate. Place the crumbs and salt on a sheet of wax paper.

3. Dip the onion rings into the egg white mixture then into the crumb mixture. Arrange the rings on the baking sheet; spray lightly with nonstick spray. Bake on the rack on the second rung of the oven until the onions are tender and the coating is crisp, about 25 minutes.

PER SERVING (¾ cup): 176 Cal, 1 g Fat, 0 g Sat Fat, 0 g Trans Fat, 0 mg Chol, 416 mg Sod, 37 g Carb, 1 g Fib, 6 g Prot, 22 mg Calc. *POINTS* value: **3.**

tip To have a batch of these onion rings on hand, prepare them (but don't bake), then freeze in zip-close plastic bags. Arrange the rings on a baking sheet and bake just before you are ready to eat them.

Garlic Spaghetti Squash

Debbe Kennedy, Montara, CA

Years ago, at a Weight Watchers meeting, Debbe learned how to steam spaghetti squash and use it instead of spaghetti. She has cooked variations of it since, but was inspired to create this special recipe for a new member in her Weight Watchers group who wanted to know how to cook spaghetti squash. Its mild flavor is beautifully enhanced here by onion, garlic, and Parmesan cheese.

1 (4-pound) spaghetti squash

2 teaspoons olive oil

1 onion, finely chopped

4 garlic cloves, minced

¼ cup grated Parmesan cheese

2 tablespoons chopped
   fresh parsley

MAKES 4 SERVINGS

1. Preheat the oven to 400°F. Spray a baking dish with nonstick spray. Pierce the squash in several places with the tip of a sharp knife and place in the baking dish with ¼ cup water. Cover with foil and bake until the squash is fork-tender, about 1 hour. Cut the squash lengthwise in half and remove the seeds. Let stand until cool enough to handle, about 10 minutes. With a fork, drag through the flesh, pulling the strands apart into a large bowl.

2. Heat the oil in a very large nonstick skillet over medium heat. Add the onion and garlic; cook, stirring frequently, until tender, about 8 minutes.

3. Add the squash, cheese, and parsley. Cook, stirring occasionally, until heated through.

PER SERVING (1¼ cups): 115 Cal, 4 g Fat, 1 g Sat Fat, 0 g Trans Fat, 4 mg Chol, 131 mg Sod, 17 g Carb, 4 g Fib, 4 g Prot, 126 mg Calc. *POINTS* value: *2.*

tip Uncut spaghetti squash can be stored at room temperature for about a month. After cutting, it will keep in the refrigerator for up to two days.

SIDE DISHES

Cranberry Sauerkraut

Linda E. Riederer, Buffalo, NY

Linda and her husband, a retired fire department chief, created this simple, yet different, side dish full of great tangy flavors. For a tad more sweetness, try dried cherries in place of the cranberries.

1 tablespoon canola oil

1 onion, finely chopped

1 Granny Smith apple, cored and chopped

¼ cup dried cranberries

1 (16-ounce) bag sauerkraut, rinsed and drained

¼ cup low-sodium chicken broth

MAKES 6 SERVINGS

1. Heat the oil in a large nonstick skillet over medium-high heat. Add the onion and cook until softened, about 6 minutes. Add the apple and cranberries; cook, stirring occasionally, until the apple begins to brown and the cranberries are softened, about 6 minutes.

2. Add the sauerkraut and broth; bring to a boil. Reduce the heat and simmer, covered, until the liquid has evaporated and the sauerkraut is tender, about 20 minutes.

PER SERVING (½ cup): 75 Cal, 3 g Fat, 0 g Sat Fat, 0 g Trans Fat, 0 mg Chol, 491 mg Sod, 13 g Carb, 4 g Fib, 1 g Prot, 32 mg Calc. *POINTS* value: **1**.

tip To keep the sodium count down, be sure to rinse and drain the sauerkraut well.

Scrumptious Stuffed Peppers

Bobbie Jessup, Tracy, CA

Like Bobbie, many of us are looking for dishes that are healthy, low in **POINTS** value, and satisfying. "These stuffed peppers seem to fit all those requirements," she says, "and I always get asked for the recipe." The flavorful filling can also be used as a stuffing for eggplant, yellow squash, or tomatoes.

2 teaspoons olive oil

1 onion, finely chopped

1 zucchini, diced

2 garlic cloves, minced

1 (14½-ounce) can no-salt-added diced tomatoes

¼ cup plain dry bread crumbs

8 kalamata olives, pitted and chopped

2 green bell peppers, cut lengthwise in half and seeded

1 (8-ounce) can no-salt-added tomato sauce

MAKES 4 SERVINGS

1. Heat the oil in a large nonstick skillet over medium-high heat. Add the onion, zucchini, and garlic; cook, stirring frequently, until tender and lightly browned, about 6 minutes. Add the diced tomatoes; bring to a boil. Reduce the heat and simmer, uncovered, until the tomatoes are softened and most of the liquid has evaporated, about 5 minutes. Remove from the heat and stir in the bread crumbs and olives.

2. Preheat the oven to 375°F.

3. Fill each pepper half with one-fourth (about ½ cup) of the onion mixture. Spoon the tomato sauce on the bottom of a 7 x 11-inch baking dish. Place the stuffed peppers on top of the sauce. Cover with foil and bake until the filling is hot and the bell peppers are tender, about 25 minutes.

PER SERVING (1 stuffed pepper): 147 Cal, 5 g Fat, 1 g Sat Fat, 0 g Trans Fat, 0 mg Chol, 244 mg Sod, 23 g Carb, 5 g Fib, 3 g Prot, 58 mg Calc. *POINTS* value: *3.*

SIDE DISHES

Green Chili Pie

Lilly-Anne Bise, Drake, CO

Lifetime member Lilly-Anne reached her goal weight six months before her wedding—and maintained that weight for the important day. "In recent months, I gained a bit and am currently 5 pounds over goal," she writes. "However, I know that for me attending meetings is the key and I'll be back at goal very soon." Enjoy this simple pie topped with salsa, fat-free sour cream, and chopped fresh cilantro for brunch or—as Lilly-Anne often does—cold in a packed lunch.

¾ cup all-purpose flour

1 cup fat-free milk

¼ cup fat-free egg substitute

1 (4½-ounce) can chopped mild green chiles

¼ cup shredded reduced-fat cheddar cheese

1 teaspoon taco seasoning

MAKES 6 SERVINGS

1. Preheat the oven to 425°F. Spray a 9-inch pie plate with nonstick spray.

2. Place the flour in a large bowl. Make a well in the center. Slowly whisk the milk and egg substitute into the center until well blended. Stir in the chiles, cheese, and taco seasoning. Scrape the mixture into the pie plate. Bake, uncovered, until slightly puffed and cooked through, about 25 minutes. Let cool 10 minutes, then cut into 6 slices.

PER SERVING (1 slice): 100 Cal, 1 g Fat, 1 g Sat Fat, 0 g Trans Fat, 4 mg Chol, 105 mg Sod, 16 g Carb, 1 g Fib, 6 g Prot, 89 mg Calc. *POINTS* value: *2.*

Sweet 'n Spicy Baked Beans

Debbe Kennedy, Montara, CA

Debbe was struggling with her weight so she decided to start cooking more healthfully, more often. She rarely ate beans until she learned that "they are a great source of protein and fiber, and best of all, they are really satisfying." It wasn't long before she created these delicious barbecued beans. She likes to serve them with barbecued chicken or on salad greens for lunch.

2 teaspoons olive oil

1 onion, finely chopped

1 green bell pepper, seeded and diced

1 (15½-ounce) can black beans, rinsed and drained

1 (15-ounce) can red kidney beans, rinsed and drained

1 (15-ounce) can pinto beans, rinsed and drained

1 cup prepared barbecue sauce

2 tablespoons spicy brown mustard

1 tablespoon packed brown sugar

1 tablespoon chili powder

MAKES 8 SERVINGS

1. Preheat the oven to 375°F. Spray a 2½-quart baking dish with nonstick spray.

2. Heat the oil in a nonstick skillet over medium-high heat. Add the onion and bell pepper; cook, stirring frequently, until tender, about 6 minutes. Transfer to a large bowl. Add the black, red, and pinto beans, the barbecue sauce, mustard, sugar, and chili powder; mix well.

3. Spoon the bean mixture into the baking dish. Bake, covered, 45 minutes. Uncover and bake until the beans are thickened slightly and bubbly, about 15 minutes longer.

PER SERVING (generous ½ cup): 149 Cal, 2 g Fat, 0 g Sat Fat, 0 g Trans Fat, 0 mg Chol, 614 mg Sod, 25 g Carb, 7 g Fib, 7 g Prot, 48 mg Calc. *POINTS* value: *2.*

tip This dish can be made up to three days ahead of time and kept, covered, in the refrigerator. To add a little more heat, add a few drops of hot pepper sauce.

SIDE DISHES

BROWN SUGAR AND
CURRY-GLAZED PINEAPPLE

Brown Sugar and Curry–Glazed Pineapple

Crystal Ralph-Haughn, Bartlesville, OK

Crystal loves to serve these delicious pineapple rings as an accompaniment to grilled or broiled ham steaks, chicken, or fish. Save yourself the trouble of slicing fresh pineapple. Packaged, fresh-cut pineapple is available in the produce section of most supermarkets.

2 tablespoons packed light brown sugar

1 teaspoon butter, at room temperature

½ teaspoon curry powder

6 (½-inch-thick) slices fresh pineapple

MAKES 8 SERVINGS

1. Combine the sugar, butter, and curry powder in a small bowl until blended. Spread the mixture on both sides of each pineapple slice.

2. Spray a large nonstick skillet with nonstick spray and set over medium-high heat. Add the pineapple slices and cook until fragrant and browned, 1–2 minutes. Flip and cook the second sides until browned, about 1 minute.

PER SERVING (2 pineapple slices): 102 Cal, 2 g Fat, 1 g Sat Fat, 0 g Trans Fat, 3 mg Chol, 5 mg Sod, 23 g Carb, 2 g Fib, 1 g Prot, 18 mg Calc. *POINTS* value: **2.**

tip We think fresh pineapple is best here, but if canned pineapple is more convenient, select sliced pineapple packed in natural juices. Be sure to pat the canned pineapple with paper towels to remove the excess moisture. This will help the sugar coating to caramelize.

CHAPTER 5

Desserts and Baked Goods

FAMILY FAVORITES AND ELEGANT ENDINGS

Rosemary-Scented Citrus Cookies

Janice Elder, Charlotte, NC

A hint of rosemary and citrus in tender cream cheese dough give Janice's winning cookies their taste of distinction. With a *POINTS* value of only 2 per serving, they can help keep us all on track.

2½ cups all-purpose flour

1 teaspoon baking powder

1 cup + 2 tablespoons sugar

6 tablespoons margarine

3 ounces fat-free
   cream cheese

1 large egg

1 teaspoon grated lemon zest

1 teaspoon grated lime zest

1 tablespoon fresh lemon juice

1 tablespoon fresh lime juice

2 teaspoons chopped
   fresh rosemary

MAKES 36 SERVINGS

1. Preheat the oven to 350°F.

2. Combine the flour and baking powder in a small bowl.

3. With an electric mixer on high speed, beat 1 cup of the sugar, the margarine, and cream cheese until light and fluffy. Add the egg, lemon and lime zests, lemon and lime juices, and rosemary. With the mixer on low speed, stir in the flour mixture until it is just moistened.

4. Shape the dough into 36 (1-inch) balls and place 2 inches apart on ungreased baking sheets. Sprinkle the remaining 2 tablespoons sugar on a sheet of wax paper. Spray the bottom of a glass with nonstick spray. Dip the glass into the sugar and use to flatten the balls into 2-inch rounds. Repeat dipping glass into the sugar and flatten each one.

5. Bake until the cookies are lightly browned at the edges, 10–12 minutes. Transfer to a rack to cool completely.

PER SERVING (1 cookie): 77 Cal, 2 g Fat, 0 g Sat Fat, 0 g Trans Fat, 6 mg Chol, 48 mg Sod, 13 g Carb, 0 g Fib, 1 g Prot, 10 mg Calc. *POINTS* value: *2.*

ROSEMARY-SCENTED
CITRUS COOKIES

DOUBLE-CHOCOLATE
BANANA CAKE

Double-Chocolate Banana Cake

Jan Beattie, Port Jefferson, NY

Jan, who has lost 26 pounds while on Weight Watchers, says, "People are surprised that I can still eat the same foods while on the program. I tell them I watch my portion sizes and make lower-fat food choices." This low-fat, dark, moist cake is a favorite of her boyfriend (who is allergic to eggs) and many of her other friends. You can serve it unadorned or with a scoop of fat-free frozen yogurt or fresh berries.

2 cups all-purpose flour

1 cup sugar

2 tablespoons unsweetened cocoa powder

½ teaspoon baking soda

½ teaspoon salt

1 large ripe banana, mashed (about ½ cup)

¾ cup canola oil

1 tablespoon fresh lemon juice

1 teaspoon vanilla extract

¾ cup fat-free milk

½ cup semisweet chocolate chips

MAKES 16 SERVINGS

1. Preheat the oven to 350°F. Spray an 8-inch square baking pan with nonstick spray.

2. Combine the flour, sugar, cocoa, baking soda, and salt in a large bowl. Combine the banana, oil, lemon juice, and vanilla in a medium bowl; stir in the milk. Add the banana mixture to the flour mixture; stir until all the flour is moistened. Stir in the chocolate chips until just blended.

3. Pour the batter into the baking pan. Bake until a toothpick inserted in the center comes out almost clean, 40–45 minutes. Cool the cake in the pan on a rack 10 minutes; remove from the pan and cool completely on the rack. Cut into 16 pieces.

PER SERVING (1 piece): 174 Cal, 5 g Fat, 1 g Sat Fat, 0 g Trans Fat, 0 mg Chol, 119 mg Sod, 30 g Carb, 1 g Fib, 2 g Prot, 20 mg Calc. **POINTS** value: 4.

DESSERTS AND BAKED GOODS

Fat-Free Chocolate Cake

Cate Whitcomb, Evanston, IL

Cate likes to serve her husband healthy, balanced meals, including desserts. She tops this winning, moist cake with fat-free whipped topping and a sprinkling of unsweetened cocoa powder. She also uses cake flour, which gives the cake a very tender crumb.

1¾ cups cake flour (not self-rising)

¾ cup sugar

½ cup unsweetened cocoa powder

½ teaspoon baking soda

¼ teaspoon salt

1 cup fat-free milk

½ cup unsweetened applesauce

2 egg whites

2 teaspoons vanilla extract

1 cup boiling water

MAKES 24 SERVINGS

1. Preheat the oven to 350°F. Spray a 9 x 13-inch baking pan with nonstick spray.

2. Combine the flour, sugar, cocoa, baking soda, and salt in a large bowl. Combine the milk, applesauce, egg whites, and vanilla in another bowl. Add the milk mixture to the flour mixture. Gradually add the boiling water and stir until just smooth. The batter will be thin.

3. Pour the batter into the pan. Bake until a toothpick inserted in the center comes out almost clean, about 30 minutes. Cool the cake in the pan on a rack 10 minutes; remove from the pan and cool completely on the rack. Cut into 24 pieces.

PER SERVING (1 piece): 65 Cal, 0 g Fat, 0 g Sat Fat, 0 g Trans Fat, 0 mg Chol, 61 mg Sod, 15 g Carb, 1 g Fib, 2 g Prot, 16 mg Calc. *POINTS* value: *1.*

Fat-Free Chocolate Zucchini Cake

Kay Biese, Chilton, WI

Weight Watchers member Kay continues to lose weight on the program. "Exercise, journaling, and meetings are a must," she says. This low-fat cake helps, too, and Kay feels she can eat a filling portion and not feel deprived. Zucchini is frequently used in quick bread and muffin recipes, but Kay has successfully added it to her recipe for chocolate cake. If you like, serve dusted with confectioners' sugar.

2 cups all-purpose flour

1 cup sugar

½ cup unsweetened cocoa powder

½ teaspoon baking soda

½ teaspoon salt

1 cup fat-free milk

½ cup unsweetened applesauce

½ cup fat-free egg substitute

2 teaspoons vanilla extract

2 cups grated zucchini

MAKES 24 SERVINGS

1. Preheat the oven to 350°F. Spray a 9 x 13-inch baking pan with nonstick spray.

2. Combine the flour, sugar, cocoa, baking soda, and salt in a large bowl. Combine the milk, applesauce, egg substitute, and vanilla in another bowl. Add the milk mixture to the flour mixture. Add the zucchini and stir until just blended.

3. Pour the batter into the pan. Bake until a toothpick inserted in the center comes out clean, about 30 minutes. Cool the cake in the pan on a rack 10 minutes; remove from pan and cool completely on rack. Cut into 24 pieces.

PER SERVING (1 piece): 85 Cal, 0 g Fat, 0 g Sat Fat, 0 g Trans Fat, 0 mg Chol, 92 mg Sod, 19 g Carb, 1 g Fib, 2 g Prot, 20 mg Calc. *POINTS* value: 2.

tip One large zucchini (about 8 ounces) will yield about 2 cups grated zucchini.

DESSERTS AND BAKED GOODS

Mock Macaroon Cake

Peggy Pappa, Lakewood, NJ

"I took this cake to a party so I could have dessert," writes Peggy. "The table was full of other fattening desserts, but before I could turn around my cake was almost gone, while the others were barely touched." Now Peggy can show off and share her winning—and unbelievably easy—recipe.

1 (16-ounce) box fat-free angel food cake mix

1 (20-ounce) can crushed pineapple, in unsweetened pineapple juice

½ cup shredded sweetened coconut

½ teaspoon ground ginger

MAKES 20 SERVINGS

1. Preheat the oven to 350°F.

2. Combine the cake mix, pineapple with its liquid, the coconut, and ginger in a large bowl. Pour the batter into an ungreased 9 x 13-inch baking dish. Bake until golden brown and a toothpick inserted in the center comes out clean, about 45 minutes. Cool the cake completely in the dish on a rack. Cut into 20 pieces.

PER SERVING (1 piece): 113 Cal, 1 g Fat, 1 g Sat Fat, 0 g Trans Fat, 0 mg Chol, 174 mg Sod, 25 g Carb, 0 g Fib, 2 g Prot, 32 mg Calc. *POINTS* value: 2.

tip It's best to use a long serrated knife to cut this cake. Before each cut, dip the blade into hot water, then wipe dry with a clean towel.

Blueberry Coffee Cake

Lori Anne Flory, Palermo, CA

Lori Anne, who has lost over 40 pounds so far on the program, was determined to make a low-calorie version of an old family favorite coffeecake. After a little experimenting, she settled on this delicious version, which "even the men agree tastes as good as the original," says Lori Anne. If fresh blueberries are not available, frozen blueberries work just as well—you can add them to the batter while still frozen. For a different twist, add 2 teaspoons of grated lemon zest and 2 teaspoons of chopped crystallized ginger to the batter.

1¾ cups all-purpose flour

½ cup granulated sugar

1½ teaspoons baking powder

⅛ teaspoon ground cloves

½ cup fat-free milk

¼ cup fat-free egg substitute

¼ cup unsweetened applesauce

2 teaspoons canola oil

1 cup fresh blueberries

2 tablespoons butter, softened

1 tablespoon packed brown sugar

½ teaspoon cinnamon

MAKES 12 SERVINGS

1. Preheat the oven to 350°F. Spray an 8-inch square baking pan with nonstick spray.

2. Combine 1½ cups of the flour, the granulated sugar, baking powder, and cloves in a large bowl. Combine the milk, egg substitute, applesauce, and oil in another bowl. Add the milk mixture to the flour mixture; stir until just blended. Stir in the blueberries. Pour batter into the pan.

3. Combine the remaining ¼ cup flour, the butter, brown sugar, and cinnamon in a small bowl until crumbs form. Sprinkle over the batter.

4. Bake until the topping is golden, the edges are lightly browned, and a toothpick inserted in the center comes out almost clean, about 30 minutes. Cool the cake in the pan on a rack 10 minutes; remove from the pan and cool completely on the rack. Cut into 12 pieces.

PER SERVING (1 piece): 142 Cal, 3 g Fat, 1 g Sat Fat, 0 g Trans Fat, 5 mg Chol, 65 mg Sod, 26 g Carb, 1 g Fib, 3 g Prot, 31 mg Calc. *POINTS* value: **3.**

DESSERTS AND BAKED GOODS

Lemon Pudding Cake

Donna Childs, New York, NY

Donna says she gets a lot of positive feedback from family and friends about this pudding cake because it tastes like comfort food. "This cake is a real treat for me." Consider serving this bar-like cake alongside a scoop of raspberry or, for a double dose of citrus, lemon sorbet.

¼ cup all-purpose flour

¼ cup sugar

1 teaspoon grated lemon zest

3 egg yolks

¼ cup fresh lemon juice

2 tablespoons margarine

3 egg whites

MAKES 12 SERVINGS

1. Preheat the oven to 350°F.

2. Combine the flour, 2 tablespoons of the sugar, and the lemon zest in a large bowl.

3. Combine the egg yolks, lemon juice, and margarine in another bowl. Add the egg yolk mixture to the flour mixture and stir until just blended. Set the batter aside.

4. With an electric mixer on low speed, beat the egg whites in a large bowl until frothy. Increase the speed to medium and add the remaining 2 tablespoons sugar, 1 tablespoon at a time, until shiny, soft peaks form. Using a large rubber spatula, gently fold the egg whites, one-third at a time, into the batter. Pour the batter into an ungreased 8-inch square baking pan. Bake, uncovered, until the cake pulls slightly away from the sides of the pan, 35–40 minutes. Let the cake cool on a rack 10 minutes, then serve warm. Cut into 12 pieces.

PER SERVING (1 piece): 63 Cal, 3 g Fat, 1 g Sat Fat, 0 g Trans Fat, 53 mg Chol, 38 mg Sod, 7 g Carb, 0 g Fib, 2 g Prot, 8 mg Calc. *POINTS* value: *2.*

tip More like a pudding than a cake, this dessert is best eaten warm or at room temperature.

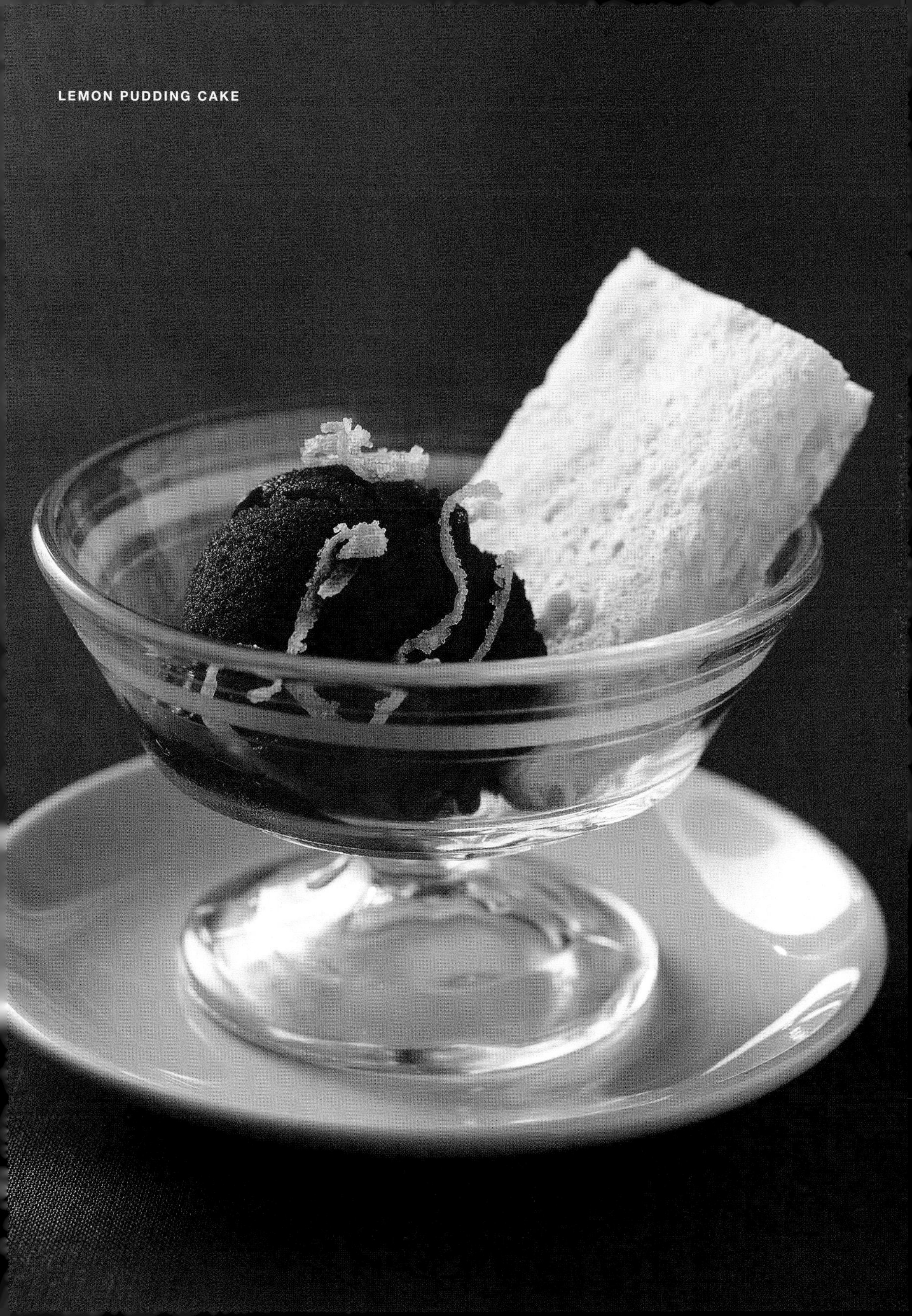
LEMON PUDDING CAKE

Chocolate Soufflé Cakes

Mary Lou Warren, Medford, OR

Lifetime member Mary Lou loves chocolate and often serves these light and lovely individual soufflés at special lunches or dinners.

6 tablespoons sugar

¼ cup unsweetened
   cocoa powder

2 tablespoons all-purpose flour

3 tablespoons very hot water

2 egg yolks

½ teaspoon vanilla extract

3 egg whites

¾ cup seedless raspberry
   fruit topping

MAKES 6 SERVINGS

1. Preheat the oven to 375°F. Spray six 6-ounce custard cups with nonstick spray. Sprinkle 2 tablespoons of the sugar into one of the molds, turning to coat bottom and sides. Toss the sugar remaining in the mold into next mold, and repeat until all molds are coated with sugar.

2. Whisk together cocoa, flour, and water in a large bowl until smooth. Add egg yolks, vanilla, and 2 tablespoons of remaining sugar, and whisk.

3. With an electric mixer on high speed, beat egg whites until foamy. Beat in the remaining 2 tablespoons sugar until shiny soft peaks form.

4. With a spatula, fold the beaten whites into the cocoa mixture, one-third at a time, until blended.

5. Spoon batter into the custard cups, filling each about half full. Arrange cups in a roasting pan. Place pan in oven, then carefully fill roasting pan with hot water until it reaches two-thirds up sides of custard cups. Bake until the soufflés are lightly browned and puffed, about 20 minutes. Carefully remove the custard cups from the water bath. Serve at once with raspberry topping.

PER SERVING (1 soufflé with 2 tablespoons raspberry topping): 151 Cal, 2 g Fat, 1 g Sat Fat, 0 g Trans Fat, 71 mg Chol, 37 mg Sod, 29 g Carb, 1 g Fib, 3 g Prot, 13 mg Calc. *POINTS* value: 3.

DESSERTS AND BAKED GOODS

Apple-Streusel Cupcakes

Tamara Carrington, Rupert, ID

High school teacher Tamara has lost an amazing 94 pounds on the Weight Watchers program and is a Lifetime member. She first made these cupcakes for a colleague's birthday and now makes them all the time. She sometimes varies her recipe by using chopped fresh peaches or drained canned crushed pineapple instead of the apples.

1 (18.25-ounce) box spice
cake mix

1 cup water

¼ cup unsweetened
applesauce

3 egg whites

2 tablespoons canola oil

1 Granny Smith apple, peeled,
cored, and finely chopped

6 tablespoons packed light
brown sugar

MAKES 18 SERVINGS

1. Preheat the oven to 350°F. Spray 18 muffin pan cups with nonstick spray.

2. With an electric mixer on medium speed, beat the cake mix, water, applesauce, egg whites, and oil in a large bowl until just blended. Fold the apple into the batter.

3. Spoon batter into the cups, filling each about two-thirds full. Sprinkle each cupcake with 1 teaspoon of brown sugar. Bake until topping is golden brown and a toothpick inserted in a cupcake comes out clean, 18–20 minutes. Cool the cupcakes in the pans on a rack 5 minutes; remove from the pans and cool completely on the rack.

PER SERVING (1 cupcake): 161 Cal, 5 g Fat, 1 g Sat Fat, 0 g Trans Fat, 8 mg Chol, 230 mg Sod, 27 g Carb, 0 g Fib, 2 g Prot, 21 mg Calc. **POINTS** value: **4.**

tip Use foil or paper liners instead of spraying the muffin cups with nonstick spray. You won't have to cool the cupcakes in the pan before removing them and cleanup is a bit easier. Store the cooled cupcakes in an airtight container at room temperature for up to three days. Or wrap and freeze the cupcakes for up to three months.

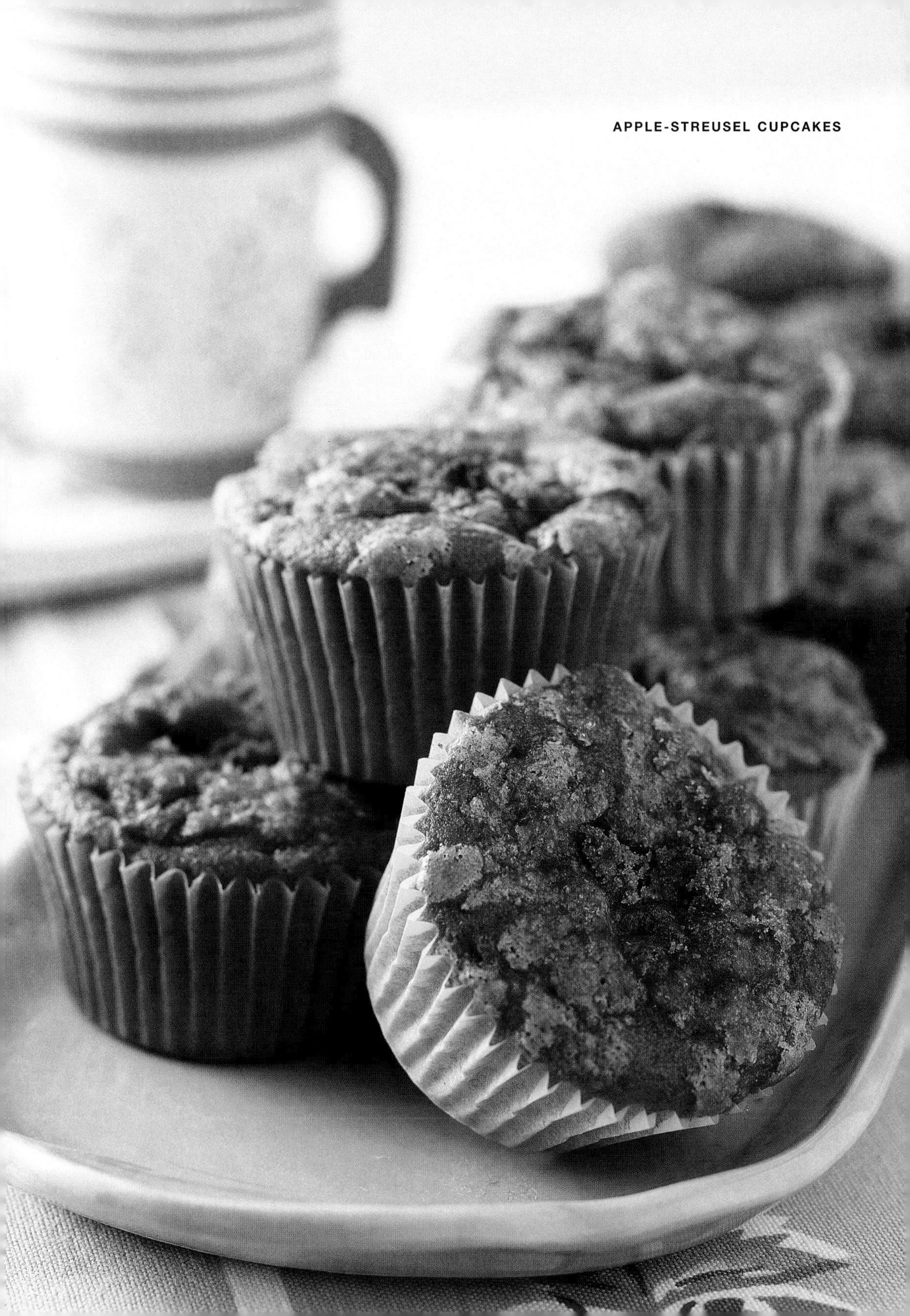

APPLE-STREUSEL CUPCAKES

Double-Layer Cheesecake

Susan K. Miller, Tempe, AZ

Susan writes, "When my mother and I both joined Weight Watchers, I decided to trim our favorite cheesecake recipe. Since then, I've made it for many friends who cannot believe it's reduced-fat!" Susan likes the cake because it's simple to make and the servings are generous.

1 cup fat-free sour cream

3 tablespoons + ½ cup sugar

1½ teaspoons vanilla extract

8 ounces fat-free
cream cheese

⅓ cup fat-free egg substitute

2 teaspoons fresh lemon juice

1 (6-ounce) prepared reduced-
fat graham cracker pie crust

MAKES 10 SERVINGS

1. Preheat the oven to 350°F.

2. Combine the sour cream, 3 tablespoons of the sugar and 1 teaspoon of the vanilla in a small bowl; set aside.

3. With an electric mixer on medium speed, beat the cream cheese and the remaining ½ cup sugar in a large bowl until smooth. Beat in the egg substitute, lemon juice, and the remaining ½ teaspoon vanilla until combined. Pour the filling into the crust. Bake until a knife inserted into the center of the cheesecake comes out clean, about 25 minutes. Spoon the sour cream mixture over the top of the cheesecake and bake 5 minutes longer.

4. Cool the cheesecake completely on a rack. Refrigerate until thoroughly chilled, at least 8 hours or up to 2 days before serving. Cut into 10 pieces.

PER SERVING (1 piece): 178 Cal, 3 g Fat, 1 g Sat Fat, 0 g Trans Fat, 6 mg Chol, 241 mg Sod, 31 g Carb, 0 g Fib, 6 g Prot, 77 mg Calc. *POINTS* value: 4.

Pumpkin Pudding

Dianna Robinson, Dickinson, TX

"We are a three-generation Weight Watchers family—my mother, myself, and my daughter," writes Lifetime member Dianna. Because this dessert is like a pumpkin pie without the crust, Dianna started calling it pumpkin pudding. So her family wouldn't miss the crust, she serves this homey treat with graham crackers.

1 (15-ounce) can solid-pack pumpkin puree

1 cup fat-free milk

⅓ cup packed light brown sugar

1 large egg

2 egg whites

1 teaspoon cinnamon

½ teaspoon ground ginger

¼ teaspoon ground cloves

MAKES 4 SERVINGS

1. Preheat the oven to 350°F. Spray an 8-inch square baking dish with nonstick spray.

2. With an electric mixer on medium speed, beat the pumpkin, milk, sugar, egg, egg whites, cinnamon, ginger, and cloves in a large bowl until smooth. Pour the pumpkin mixture into the dish. Bake, uncovered, until the filling is set and a knife inserted into the center comes out clean, about 40 minutes. Cool completely on a rack. Refrigerate, covered, at least 3 hours before serving.

PER SERVING (¾ cup): 156 Cal, 2 g Fat, 1 g Sat Fat, 0 g Trans Fat, 54 mg Chol, 87 mg Sod, 30 g Carb, 5 g Fib, 7 g Prot, 124 mg Calc. *POINTS* value: 2.

MOCHA CREAM PIE

Mocha Cream Pie

Kate Hare, Alameda, CA

Kate feels that the knowledge she has gained from being a Weight Watchers member has not only helped her lose weight, but she has been able to advise her husband and two sons at various times when they needed to shed a few pounds. Kate says, "I love making desserts, but feel responsible for making them healthy for my family." This pie deliciously fills the bill.

¼ cup sugar

¼ cup unsweetened
    cocoa powder

2 tablespoons all-purpose flour

1 tablespoon instant espresso
    coffee powder

2 cups fat-free milk

1 large egg, lightly beaten

1 teaspoon vanilla extract

1 (6-ounce) prepared reduced-
    fat graham cracker pie crust

4 teaspoons pasteurized egg
    white powder

¼ cup warm water

½ cup reduced-fat non-dairy
    whipped topping

MAKES 8 SERVINGS

1. Combine the sugar, cocoa, flour, and instant espresso in a medium saucepan. Whisk in the milk and egg. Cook over medium-low heat, stirring constantly, until the mixture just coats the back of a spoon, about 8 minutes (do not boil, or the mixture may curdle). Remove from the heat, then stir in the vanilla. Spoon the filling into the pie crust; let cool 30 minutes. Refrigerate, covered, until the filling is set, about 2 hours.

2. To make the meringue, combine the egg white powder and warm water in a medium bowl. Using a fork, gently stir until the powder absorbs the water, about 2 minutes. Continue to stir until completely dissolved, about 1 minute longer. With an electric mixer on medium-high speed, beat the egg white powder mixture in a medium bowl until soft peaks form. Gently fold in the whipped topping.

3. Uncover the pie, then spoon the meringue mixture evenly over the top. Refrigerate up to 8 hours, until readyto serve. Cut into 8 pieces.

PER SERVING (1 piece): 176 Cal, 5 g Fat, 2 g Sat Fat, 1 g Trans Fat, 28 mg Chol, 141 mg Sod, 28 g Carb, 1 g Fib, 6 g Prot, 83 mg Calc. *POINTS* value: **4.**

DESSERTS AND BAKED GOODS

Pumpkin Patch Pudding

Pamela Sheridan, Essex Junction, VT

"Autumn is a wonderful season in Vermont and I adore all things made with pumpkin," writes Pamela. She likes to serve this chilled pudding in martini glasses with a little whipped topping and a sprinkling of freshly grated nutmeg.

1 (15-ounce) can solid-pack pumpkin puree

1 envelope (four ½-cup servings) sugar-free instant butterscotch pudding

1½ cups fat-free milk

½ cup fat-free egg substitute

1 tablespoon maple syrup

1 teaspoon cinnamon

½ teaspoon ground ginger

¼ teaspoon nutmeg

⅛ teaspoon ground cloves

MAKES 4 SERVINGS

1. Preheat the oven to 425°F. Spray an 8-inch square baking dish with nonstick spray.

2. With an electric mixer on medium speed, beat the pumpkin, instant pudding, milk, egg substitute, syrup, cinnamon, ginger, nutmeg, and cloves in a large bowl until smooth. Pour the pumpkin mixture into the baking dish. Bake, uncovered, for 10 minutes. Reduce the oven temperature to 350°F and continue baking until a knife inserted into the center comes out clean, about 30 minutes longer. Cool completely on a rack. Refrigerate, covered, at least 3 hours before serving.

PER SERVING (generous ¾ cup): 122 Cal, 1 g Fat, 0 g Sat Fat, 0 g Trans Fat, 2 mg Chol, 417 mg Sod, 23 g Carb, 5 g Fib, 8 g Prot, 152 mg Calc. *POINTS* value: 2.

tip For a change, you can drizzle the pudding with a little fat-free caramel sauce and sprinkle with crushed reduced-fat gingersnap cookies.

Sugar-and-Spice Baked Fruit

Jan Johns, Boise, ID

You can use Bartlett or Anjou pears instead of Bosc pears for this warm fruit compote, if you like. For best results, choose pears that are just ripe, but not overripe. To ripen hard pears, put them in a bowl at room temperature for two to three days.

12 pitted prunes

¼ cup water

4 firm-ripe Bosc pears, peeled and cut into 1½-inch chunks

2 tablespoons packed light brown sugar

½ teaspoon cinnamon

1 tablespoon melted butter

2 tablespoons chopped walnuts

MAKES 6 SERVINGS

1. Preheat the oven to 375°F. Spray an 8-inch square baking dish with nonstick spray.

2. Bring the prunes and water to a boil in a small saucepan. Remove from heat; let stand, covered, 10 minutes to soften.

3. Combine the pears, sugar, and cinnamon in a bowl. Add the prunes and liquid. Spoon the pear mixture into the baking dish. Drizzle the butter over the fruit, then sprinkle with the walnuts.

4. Bake, uncovered, until the pears are tender and the top is lightly browned, about 30 minutes.

PER SERVING (⅔ cup): 156 Cal, 4 g Fat, 1 g Sat Fat, 0 g Trans Fat, 5 mg Chol, 3 mg Sod, 32 g Carb, 3 g Fib, 1 g Prot, 30 mg Calc. **POINTS** value: **3.**

tip To skip the step of soaking the prunes in boiling water, use 12 ready-to-serve pitted prunes from a 16-ounce jar plus ¼ cup of the liquid.

DESSERTS AND BAKED GOODS

Streusel Baked Pears

Linda Richter, Redwood City, CA

"My husband thought I was going off my diet when I served these delicious pears for dessert," writes Linda, who likes to serve this comforting dish warm with frozen fat-free vanilla yogurt. When the fruits of summer—peaches, nectarines, and plums—abound, you can substitute them for the pears.

4 firm-ripe Bartlett pears, peeled, halved, and cored

½ cup quick-cooking rolled oats

2 tablespoons packed light brown sugar

2 tablespoons margarine

1 tablespoon all-purpose flour

1 tablespoon sliced almonds

½ teaspoon cinnamon

MAKES 8 SERVINGS

1. Preheat the oven to 375°F. Spray a 7 x 11-inch square baking dish with nonstick spray. Arrange the pears, cut-side up, in the baking dish.

2. Combine the oats, sugar, margarine, flour, almonds, and cinnamon in a small bowl until the mixture is blended and crumbly. Sprinkle over the pears.

3. Bake, uncovered, until the filling is bubbly and the top is golden, 40–50 minutes. Cool on a rack about 15 minutes, then serve warm or at room temperature.

PER SERVING (1 pear half): 132 Cal, 4 g Fat, 1 g Sat Fat, 0 g Trans Fat, 0 mg Chol, 37 mg Sod, 26 g Carb, 6 g Fib, 2 g Prot, 102 mg Calc. *POINTS* value: *2.*

Land, Sea, and Sky Dessert

Barbara Brass Duncan, Ontario, Canada

"This recipe was handed down from my grandmother," writes Barbara. It has three distinct layers that are created when the filling is poured into a glass bowl and left undisturbed. The bottom layer is a light custard, the center a pudding-like layer, and the meringue floats to the top.

2 cups fat-free milk

1 envelope unflavored gelatin

2 tablespoons sugar

2 egg yolks

1 teaspoon vanilla extract

4 teaspoons pasteurized egg
   white powder

¼ cup warm water

MAKES 4 SERVINGS

1. Place the milk in a medium saucepan. Sprinkle the gelatin over the milk; let soften 5 minutes.

2. Heat the milk mixture over medium heat. Add the sugar and egg yolks; cook, stirring frequently, until the gelatin is completely dissolved, bubbles just begin to form at the edges of the pan, and the mixture thickens slightly, about 8 minutes (do not boil or the mixture may curdle). Remove the pan from the heat; stir in the vanilla. Transfer the mixture to a large bowl.

3. Combine the egg white powder and the warm water in a medium bowl. Stir gently for 2 minutes giving the powder time to absorb the water. Continue stirring until completely dissolved, about 1 minute longer.

4. With an electric mixer on high speed, beat the egg white powder mixture until soft peaks form, about 3 minutes; gently fold into the milk mixture. Pour the mixture into a 1-quart glass bowl. Let stand, undisturbed, about 20 minutes. Cover and refrigerate until set, about 3 hours.

PER SERVING (¾ cup): 114 Cal, 3 g Fat, 1 g Sat Fat, 0 g Trans Fat, 109 mg Chol, 99 mg Sod, 13 g Carb, 0 g Fib, 9 g Prot, 165 mg Calc. *POINTS* value: **3.**

Sweet Popovers with Spicy Apple Compote

Jane Gaither, Nashville, TN

Jane usually makes this for dessert but says it's also terrific for brunch. If you like, add a few raisins or dried cranberries with a little grated orange zest to the compote.

3 Golden Delicious apples, peeled, cored, and thinly sliced

½ cup water

¼ cup + 1 teaspoon granulated sugar

1 teaspoon fresh lemon juice

1 teaspoon cinnamon

½ teaspoon ground ginger

¼ teaspoon nutmeg

⅛ teaspoon ground cloves

3 egg whites

1 cup low-fat (1%) milk

1 tablespoon canola oil

1 cup all-purpose flour

⅛ teaspoon salt

2 tablespoons confectioners' sugar

MAKES 8 SERVINGS

1. To make the compote, combine the apples, water, ¼ cup of the granulated sugar, the lemon juice, cinnamon, ginger, nutmeg, and cloves in a large saucepan; bring to a boil. Reduce the heat and simmer, covered, until the apples are very tender and any liquid has evaporated, 8–10 minutes. Remove from the heat; keep warm.

2. To make the popovers, preheat the oven to 375°F. Spray a 6-cup muffin tin with nonstick spray.

3. With an electric mixer on medium speed, beat the egg whites in a large bowl until frothy. Beat in the milk and oil. Add the flour, remaining 1 teaspoon granulated sugar, and the salt; beat until smooth. Spoon the batter into the muffin cups filling each about two-thirds full.

4. Bake 40 minutes, then with the tip of a small knife, quickly make a small slit in the top of each popover to let the steam escape; bake 5 minutes longer. Remove from the muffin cups at once.

5. Spoon the warm compote over each popover, sprinkle with the confectioners' sugar and serve.

PER SERVING (1 popover, about ⅓ cup compote, and 1 teaspoon confectioners' sugar): 208 Cal, 3 g Fat, 1 g Sat Fat, 0 g Trans Fat, 2 mg Chol, 97 mg Sod, 40 g Carb, 2 g Fib, 5 g Prot, 62 mg Calc. *POINTS* value: 4.

SWEET POPOVERS WITH
SPICY APPLE COMPOTE

Crème Victoria

Victoria Shirley, Bark River, MI

"I love whipped cream," writes Victoria, who has found a way to cleverly satisfy that love with this low-*POINTS* value, creamy dessert. And since she relies heavily on fruit products to fill her up, she often serves this custard with mashed berries that have been soaked in a little white grape juice. For special occasions, she makes it in a 2-cup ring mold and after unmolding, she mounds fresh berries in the center and garnishes it with sprigs of mint.

1 envelope unflavored gelatin
¼ cup cold water
1½ cups fat-free milk
2 tablespoons sugar
1 cup fat-free sour cream
½ teaspoon almond extract

MAKES 4 SERVINGS

1. Sprinkle the gelatin over the water in a small bowl; let soften 5 minutes.

2. Heat the milk and sugar in a small saucepan over medium heat. Add the gelatin mixture and cook, stirring frequently, until the sugar and gelatin are completely dissolved and bubbles just begin to form at the edges of the pan, about 5 minutes. Remove the pan from the heat; transfer the mixture to a large bowl. Add the sour cream and almond extract; stir until smooth. Cover and refrigerate until set, about 3 hours.

PER SERVING (¾ cup): 125 Cal, 0 g Fat, 0 g Sat Fat, 0 g Trans Fat, 12 mg Chol, 131 mg Sod, 21 g Carb, 0 g Fib, 7 g Prot, 194 mg Calc. *POINTS* value: **3.**

Summer Fantasy Pudding with Strawberry Sauce

Mary E. Reynolds, El Sobrante, CA

Mary was given a version of this delicious recipe from a friend whose family came from Latvia. To fit the Weight Watchers profile, Mary experimented until she created this creamy, pale pink pudding.

½ (16-ounce) bag frozen whole strawberries, thawed

¼ cup + 1 cup water

2 tablespoons + ¼ cup sugar

2 teaspoons cornstarch

½ cup fat-free vanilla yogurt

3 cups light cranberry juice

¼ cup fresh lemon juice

⅛ teaspoon salt

½ cup + 1 tablespoon quick-cooking farina or cream of wheat

MAKES 4 SERVINGS

1. To prepare the sauce, puree the strawberries in a food processor until smooth; set aside. Combine ¼ cup of the water, 2 tablespoons of the sugar, and the cornstarch in a saucepan until blended. Add the strawberry puree; bring to a boil. Reduce the heat and simmer, stirring constantly, until the sauce boils and thickens, about 2 minutes. Transfer the sauce to a bowl; let cool, about 30 minutes. Add the yogurt and stir until blended. Cover and refrigerate, about 30 minutes.

2. Meanwhile, to prepare the pudding, bring the cranberry juice, lemon juice, salt, the remaining 1 cup water, and the remaining ¼ cup sugar to a boil in a large saucepan. Whisk in the farina in a slow steady stream. Reduce the heat and simmer, stirring constantly with a wooden spoon, until the pudding thickens and coats the back of the spoon, about 5 minutes. Transfer the pudding to a large bowl. Let stand at room temperature until cool, about 30 minutes. With an electric mixer on high speed, beat the pudding until it turns a pale pink, about 3 minutes. Serve with the strawberry sauce.

PER SERVING (⅔ cup pudding with 3 tablespoons strawberry sauce): 127 Cal, 0 g Fat, 0 g Sat Fat, 0 g Trans Fat, 0 mg Chol, 52 mg Sod, 30 g Carb, 1 g Fib, 2 g Prot, 58 mg Calc. *POINTS* value: *2*.

DESSERTS AND BAKED GOODS

Whipped Yogurt and Tangy Berry Parfaits

Elan Monique Geiger Buendia, Chicago, IL

Elan writes, "I am from a family of inspired cooks. I learned to cook from my mom." Now Elan can boast, because *she* gave this recipe to her mom—and to us. It's a truly inspiring celebration of fresh berries in season.

5 strawberries, cut into quarters

½ cup blueberries

½ cup raspberries

½ cup blackberries

2 tablespoons chopped fresh mint

1 tablespoon maple syrup

1 cup fat-free vanilla yogurt

½ cup fat-free non-dairy whipped topping

¼ cup low-fat granola

Mint sprigs

MAKES 4 SERVINGS

1. Combine the strawberries, blueberries, raspberries, blackberries, chopped mint, and the maple syrup in a medium bowl.

2. Combine the yogurt and whipped topping in another bowl. Alternately layer the berry mixture with the yogurt mixture, ending with the berries, in four 6-ounce parfait glasses. Sprinkle each with a tablespoon of the granola and garnish with the mint sprigs.

PER SERVING (1 parfait): 145 Cal, 1 g Fat, 0 g Sat Fat, 0 g Trans Fat, 1 mg Chol, 66 mg Sod, 31 g Carb, 4 g Fib, 4 g Prot, 134 mg Calc. *POINTS* value: 2.

tip For a change of pace, you can use raspberry or mango sorbet instead of the yogurt.

Granola Cookies

Susan K. McClure, Denver, IA

"After my Dad's heart attack, my mother modified many of our favorite recipes to fit his new diet. This cookie is a favorite of mine, so we adjusted it, substituting a little oil for a lot of butter," says Susan, who often has two of these cookies for a quick breakfast or one as a snack.

1¾ cups all-purpose flour

1¾ teaspoons baking powder

½ teaspoon salt

¾ cup granulated sugar

¼ cup packed brown sugar

3 tablespoons canola oil

1 large egg

1 teaspoon vanilla extract

1 cup low-fat granola
   with raisins

MAKES 24 SERVINGS

1. Preheat the oven to 350°F. Spray 2 baking sheets with nonstick spray.

2. Combine the flour, baking powder, and salt in a small bowl; set aside.

3. With an electric mixer on high speed, beat the granulated sugar, brown sugar, and oil until light and fluffy. Add the egg and vanilla; beat well. With the mixer on low speed, stir in the flour mixture until all of the flour is just moistened. Stir in the granola.

4. Drop the dough by rounded teaspoons, 2 inches apart, onto the baking sheets, making a total of 24 cookies. Bake until almost set and light golden, 10–12 minutes. Cool on the baking sheets on racks until firm, about 5 minutes. Remove the cookies from the baking sheets and cool completely on the racks.

PER SERVING (1 cookie): 98 Cal, 2 g Fat, 0 g Sat Fat, 0 g Trans Fat, 9 mg Chol, 89 mg Sod, 18 g Carb, 0 g Fib, 2 g Prot, 12 mg Calc. *POINTS* value: 2.

DESSERTS AND BAKED GOODS

GRANOLA COOKIES, CHOCOLATE MERINGUE COOKIES, AND ANGEL PEAK COOKIES

Chocolate Meringue Cookies

Elizabeth Thatcher, Plaucheville, LA

Elizabeth has been a Lifetime member for almost three decades. She makes these cookies to have on hand for herself all the time. "I like being able to have six cookies and know that they are low in *POINTS* value," she writes.

3 egg whites, at room
   temperature
¼ teaspoon cream of tartar
2 tablespoons sugar-free
   instant chocolate
   pudding mix
¼ cup sugar

MAKES 6 SERVINGS

1. Preheat oven to 225°F. Line 2 large baking sheets with foil.

2. With an electric mixer on medium speed, beat the egg whites and cream of tartar in a large bowl until frothy. Beat in the instant pudding. Gradually beat in the sugar, 2 tablespoons at a time, until the sugar completely dissolves and the egg whites stand in stiff, glossy peaks, about 6 minutes.

3. Drop the meringue by rounded teaspoons, ½-inch apart, onto the baking sheets, making a total of 36 cookies. Bake until they feel crisp to the touch, about 2 hours. Turn the oven off and leave the meringues in the oven until they are crisp and dry to the touch, about 1 hour longer.

4. Carefully loosen the meringues from the foil, then transfer to a rack to cool completely.

PER SERVING (6 meringues): 46 Cal, 0 g Fat, 0 g Sat Fat, 0 g Trans Fat, 0 mg Chol, 80 mg Sod, 10 g Carb, 0 g Fib, 2 g Prot, 2 mg Calc. *POINTS* value: *1*.

tip Before whipping egg whites, be sure they're at room temperature—they create more volume than chilled egg whites.

DESSERTS AND BAKED GOODS

Angel Peak Cookies

Susan Ardoin, Lake Charles, LA

Susan enjoys being a Weight Watchers member because she gets ideas and recipes from people at the meetings and "their new ideas are motivators," she writes. Her desire for pecan pie was the inspiration behind these heavenly cookies.

3 egg whites, at room temperature

¼ teaspoon cream of tartar

3 tablespoons sugar

½ teaspoon vanilla extract

24 salt crackers, coarsely crumbled (1 cup)

¼ cup finely chopped pecans

MAKES 18 SERVINGS

1. Preheat heat the oven to 325°F. Line a large baking sheet with foil.

2. With an electric mixer on medium speed, beat the egg whites and the cream of tartar in a large bowl until just frothy. Gradually beat in the sugar, 1 tablespoon at a time, until the sugar completely dissolves and the egg whites stand in soft, glossy peaks, about 5 minutes. Beat in the vanilla. With a rubber spatula, gently fold in the cracker crumbs and pecans until just blended.

3. Drop the batter by rounded tablespoons, ½-inch apart, onto the baking sheet, making a total of 18 cookies. Bake until they feel dry to the touch, and the tops are lightly browned, 18–20 minutes.

4. Carefully loosen the cookies from the foil, then transfer to a rack to cool completely.

PER SERVING (1 cookie): 40 Cal, 2 g Fat, 0 g Sat Fat, 0 g Trans Fat, 0 mg Chol, 60 mg Sod, 5 g Carb, 0 g Fib, 1 g Prot, 6 mg Calc. *POINTS* value: *1.*

About Our Recipes

We make every effort to ensure that you will have success with our recipes. For best results and for nutritional accuracy, please keep the following guidelines in mind:

• All recipes feature approximate nutritional information; our recipes are analyzed for Calories (Cal), Total Fat (Fat), Saturated Fat (Sat Fat), Trans Fat (Trans Fat), Cholesterol (Chol), Sodium (Sod), Carbohydrates (Carb), Dietary Fiber (Fib), Protein (Prot), and Calcium (Calc).

• Nutritional information for recipes that include meat, fish, and poultry are based on cooked skinless boneless portions (unless otherwise stated), with the fat trimmed as specified in the recipe.

• All recipes include *POINTS* values based on the Weight Watchers **FlexPoints** Food System. *POINTS* values are calculated from a proprietary formula that takes into account calories, total fat, and dietary fiber.

• Before serving, divide foods—including any vegetables, sauce, or accompaniments—into portions of equal size according to the designated number of servings per recipe.

• Any substitutions made to the ingredients will alter the "Per serving" nutritional information and may affect the *POINTS* value.

• Additionally, substituting fat-free foods for any low-fat ingredients specified in a recipe may affect the consistency, texture, or flavor of the finished dish.

• If you prefer to avoid using alcohol in any recipe, you may substitute an equal amount of water, broth, or juice.

• It is implied that all greens in recipes should be washed or rinsed.

• All herbs called for are fresh, not dried, unless otherwise specified.

Dry and Liquid
Measurement Equivalents

If you are converting the recipes in this book to metric measurements,
use the following chart as a guide.

TEASPOONS	TABLESPOONS	CUPS	FLUID OUNCES
3 teaspoons	1 tablespoon		1/2 fluid ounce
6 teaspoons	2 tablespoons	1/8 cup	1 fluid ounce
8 teaspoons	2 tablespoons plus 2 teaspoons	1/6 cup	
12 teaspoons	4 tablespoons	1/4 cup	2 fluid ounces
15 teaspoons	5 tablespoons	1/3 cup minus 1 teaspoon	
16 teaspoons	5 tablespoons plus 1 teaspoon	1/3 cup	
18 teaspoons	6 tablespoons	1/4 cup plus 2 tablespoons	3 fluid ounces
24 teaspoons	8 tablespoons	1/2 cup	4 fluid ounces
30 teaspoons	10 tablespoons	1/2 cup plus 2 tablespoons	5 fluid ounces
32 teaspoons	10 tablespoons plus 2 teaspoons	2/3 cup	
36 teaspoons	12 tablespoons	3/4 cup	6 fluid ounces
42 teaspoons	14 tablespoons	1 cup minus 1 tablespoon	7 fluid ounces
45 teaspoons	15 tablespoons	1 cup minus 1 tablespoon	
48 teaspoons	16 tablespoons	1 cup	8 fluid ounces

VOLUME	
1/4 teaspoon	1 milliliter
1/2 teaspoon	2 milliliters
1 teaspoon	5 milliliters
1 tablespoon	15 milliliters
2 tablespoons	30 milliliters
3 tablespoons	45 milliliters
1/4 cup	60 milliliters
1/3 cup	80 milliliters
1/2 cup	120 milliliters
2/3 cup	160 milliliters
3/4 cup	175 milliliters
1 cup	240 milliliters
1 quart	950 milliliters

LENGTH	
1 inch	25 millimeters
1 inch	2.5 centimeters

OVEN TEMPERATURE			
250°F	120°C	400°F	200°C
275°F	140°C	425°F	220°C
300°F	150°C	450°F	230°C
325°F	160°C	475°F	250°C
350°F	180°C	500°F	260°C
375°F	190°C	525°F	270°C

WEIGHT	
1 ounce	30 grams
1/4 pound	120 grams
1/2 pound	240 grams
1 pound	480 grams

NOTE: Measurement of less than 1/8 teaspoon is considered a dash or a
pinch. Metric volume measurements are approximate.

Index